Ideas and Suggestions to
Love and Respect
Your Husband

Teresa Shields Parker
Robert J. Vickers

Here are more than 199 ideas and suggestions
to help improve your marriage, whether
you're working together or alone
to make needed changes.

WINEPRESS WP PUBLISHING

Packaged by WinePress Publishing, PO Box 428, Enumclaw, WA 98022. The views expressed or implied in this work do not necessarily reflect those of WinePress Publishing. Ultimate design, content, and editorial accuracy of this work are the responsibilities of the authors.

Unless otherwise noted all scriptures are taken from the Holy Bible, New International Version, Copyright © 1973, 1978, 1984 by the International Bible Society. Used by permission of Zondervan Publishing House. The "NIV" and "New International Version" trademarks are registered in the United States Patent and Trademark Office by International Bible Society.

ISBN 1-57921-207-7
Library of Congress Catalog Card Number: 98-83280

Other Books

199 IDEAS AND SUGGESTIONS
TO HONOR AND LOVE YOUR WIFE

FAMILY FACTS, FAVORITES
AND FUN THINGS TO KNOW

Others in process and due to be released soon! Call for details!

1-888-857-2993
or
1-888-836-8625

To Learn more about Tentmakers
Missionary Fellowship see page 95.

Three Cautions

1. Don't love your husband in *your* love language.

2. Learn and use *your husband's* love language liberally.

3. Following a few of the ideas and suggestions in this book could change your life—and your husband's!

Teresa's Dedication

To Roy, who loves me
in spite of my faults and weaknesses
and who is the real hero
in my life and in our family!

In memory of my mother,
Donna Carr Shields;
my grandmother Maydene Carr;
and my great-grandmother Mary Jane White,
whose godly lives exemplified
love, commitment and perseverance
in the midst of everyday trials
and seemingly unbeatable odds.
I am privileged to have known them
and to have been taught by them.
They are a part of what I am today.

Bob's Dedication

To all you husbands:
Forget that your wife owns this book,
and become the husband God wants you to be.

Especially to my accountability friends and partners:
Thanks for helping me to learn how and for holding me
accountable to serve my wife and not try to change her,
not worry about how she responds
and not focus on her behavior.

And thanks to
Tentmakers Missionary Fellowship
who has made a dream become reality.
It **is** "too good to be true—but the Bible really works!"
Laura, thank you for loving me.

Acknowledgments

Special thanks to the following:

All who contributed to the content of this book, edited drafts and provided invaluable feedback:

Beth Abernathie	Roy Parker
Shirley Bishop	Bishop Phil Porter
Julie Casey	Jim and Robin Riley
John Christensen	Jeff and Dana Sharland
Gary and Doris Denbow	Phil and Cindy Shearrer
Jim and Lana Ferneau	Ernest and Diane Shields
Paul and Carolyn Fitzgerald	Debbie Short
Donna Gates	Dale and Georgia Swoboda
Kathy Glabe	Laura Vickers
Judy Hunter	Rick Vidmar
Cindy Minchew	LaVonne Way
Linda Mura	Aubrey and Kimberly Weger
Gregory and Linda Ordway	Steve and Jean Yount
Jacquieline Packham	Carl Yount, Jr.
Nancy Rebecca Palmer	Al Zechial

And thanks to the authors of books and tapes
on relationships listed in Appendix I.

Table of Contents

Introduction

This book is written to give ideas and suggestions that might help wives in their relationship with their husbands. It is not meant to be a total guide to having a great marriage. While not every idea will be helpful in every marriage, I hope that you find many helpful suggestions.

You may have additional ideas and suggestions that have benefited your own relationship. Jot them down, and send them to us. We see this as a working draft, a document in progress that will never be complete!

This book was written with input from many different women, those whose husbands range from believers, to nominal Christians, to nonbelievers. Many who shared ideas had difficulty allowing their names to be used. They didn't feel their marriage was "ideal." No marriage is. We are all travelers along the same road. None of us are perfect.

The ideas and suggestions in this book are ones we all need to hear. Don't think because I compiled this book that I am practicing every idea here. My life is also a work in progress. If there is any woman out there who is doing everything in this book, I want to hear from her and meet her. She would be the ultimate Christian wife, and all women could pattern their lives after her.

In writing this book, I struggled with the concept of submission and how to include it. My concept of submission and what has worked in my marriage of 21-plus years is to see submission as harmony. I addressed this in idea #O in "Begin by Working on Yourself." But even when singing harmony, someone has to sing lead. We've found that in certain situations, I sing lead, especially if it is a situation that involves my strengths, spiritual gifts or natural abilities. Most of the time, though, my husband sings lead in the situations that involve both of us. Sometimes I have to wait until he's ready to sing lead. And we give and take in order for the "song" to sound right. We harmonize, or at least we try.

In no way do I want any woman to read this book and think she must be a doormat to her husband and serve him continually to her own detriment. Women should have their own identity within the marriage relationship. They should work on becoming everything they can be and being all God wants them to be. However, a godly woman should be a servant and should treat those she meets with a servant's attitude. If she is not serving her husband, she is not loving him. The idea of servanthood is a Christian idea, not necessarily an idea for wives only. Galatians 5:13 says it this way: "For you, Dear Friends, have been called to live in freedom—not freedom to satisfy your sinful nature, but freedom to serve one another in love. For the whole law can be summed up in this one command: 'Love your neighbor as yourself.'"

This does not mean that women are below or above men. It simply means what it says: we are to serve each other. The elevation of women to equality with men was expressed by Paul in Galatians 3:28: "There is neither Jew nor Greek, slave nor free, male nor female, for you are all one in Christ Jesus." But in any relationship, especially a marriage that is going to last for any length of time, one person has to lead and the other follow. There cannot be two leaders.

Think about friendships you have with other women. At some point, one of you has to "sing" lead. You might make a suggestion to go shopping. Your friend might add the idea of shopping at the mall. You might agree to drive, and she might suggest eating at a sandwich shop before you get there. Who sang lead? Both of you did, but not at the same time. If you disagreed, what did you do? You didn't both sing different leads at the same time. No music is made that way. You gave in to her, or she gave in to you. If you were going to get anywhere or if any harmony was developed, one of you had to give in. If you can give in a friendship and learn how to harmonize, why not in a marriage with your husband? Don't let the thought *No man is going to tell me what to do* ruin your ability to harmonize and work out amiable solutions to everyday problems. If you disagree, defer to him. It won't kill you. You might find it freeing. And the song you sing together will be more beautiful.

Marriage failure is the norm these days. Being married for many years is unusual. I've wondered what the magic ingredient is to assurance that a marriage will survive. I've wondered if physical beauty is the answer, and yet I've seen some very attractive women—beauty queens and movie stars—fail miserably at their marriages. I've wondered if intelligence is the answer, and yet I've seen many Ph.D.s with difficult marriages. I've wondered if those who study emotions and feelings are more successful at marriage, and yet many counselors and psychologists are among those whose marriages don't survive. I've wondered if commitment to the church is the answer, and yet many very "religious" people fail in marriage, deeply wounding their spouse, children and family. I've seen all categories of successful people try and fail at marriage. And I've watched those who seemingly have little going for them remain married for years and years.

The only thread that runs through all successful marriages I've seen is that both partners really want the marriage to work. Both are committed to the best for the other person. The couples are committed to finding harmony without always having to sing a solo. Make a commitment to yourself that you will be committed to your husband's best. If you have been waiting for him to change for your marriage to get better, you're on the wrong track. You are not perfect. You have changing to do yourself.

Start with you. That's why we put the section "Begin by Working on Yourself" at the beginning of the book. As you focus on yourself, you'll begin to see changes in your relationship. Your husband may be changing, but most of the difference will be in response to changes he sees in you.

Once you start the process yourself, move on to discover other ways you can show love and respect to your husband. The book is divided into chapters that mirror some of the popular thinking about different languages or ways to express love. They include the following:

- Create and Continually Enhance Meaning and Value for Him
- Encourage, Affirm and Support Him with Your Words
- Spend Time with Him
- Serve Him in the Home
- Physically Adore, Respect and Love Him
- Give Him Gifts of Love
- Just Because You Love Him

Remember that since opposites attract, the things that seem easiest for you to do may not be the things your husband really wants or needs from you. You may be great at cleaning house and doing acts of service, but what he really wants is your undivided attention. You may be spending lots of time with him, but what he really needs is to hear words of affirmation, encouragement and support. The key here is to discover what ways your husband enjoys receiving love from you. Does he get excited about gifts, or does he feel ho-hum about them? Does he seem satisfied and content if you spend lots of time together, or does it not seem to bother him if you don't see each other for several days. Does he blossom when you praise him, or do your words pass by like he can take them or leave them? Does he notice when you clean the house, do the laundry or wash the dishes, or is his mood the same whether the house is clean or not? Does he enjoy being touched, holding hands, kissing and hugging at times other than when you are in the bedroom, or do those kinds of acts annoy or frustrate him?

If you're still not sure how your husband enjoys receiving love, think about how he enjoys showing love to you. Does he shower you with gifts when you wish he would save the money? He may be saying to you that he likes to receive gifts. Does he enjoy serving you by helping with household chores? He may be saying that serving him is the way he knows you love him. Is he always trying to plan time with you, and does he get upset if you have to be away, work long hours and don't get to see each other? He may be saying that, for him, love is spelled t-i-m-e. Does he always touch you during the day? He may be saying that he doesn't feel loved unless you are physically adoring him. Is he always praising you and encouraging you? He may be saying, *Do the same for me, and I'll know you love me.*

As you read through this book, especially chapters 2 to 6, notice the things your husband would enjoy if you did them, not necessarily just what you currently do for him or what you might enjoy doing for him.

My pastor is fond of saying, "Find one thing to work on. You can't handle more than one at a time." My suggestion to you is the same. Find one idea in this book that leaps out at you, and begin working on developing that for your husband. This book is not meant to be a way for you to check off everything you are doing or have been doing. It is meant to be just as it says in the title, a book of ideas and suggestions, things to try, ways to improve, new thoughts, different concepts. They might work for your marriage and they might not.

Read the suggestions. Mark those that hit you hardest and that you know would be most difficult for you to do. Choose at least one of these to try this week. What have you got to lose?

TERESA SHIELDS PARKER

Begin by Working on Yourself

Some days it's almost painful to watch television. The ads show women with perfect bodies. The shows star not only women with perfect bodies, hair and teeth, but also those who are intelligent and well paid—executives, attorneys, judges, television personalities or real-estate agents—and who have children and husbands and huge homes to supervise. These superwomen manage to do everything with a smile without getting a hair out of place.

Don't you wish television would more often depict a mom in a housedress and apron, at home, taking care of the house and kids? In the '50s and '60s, at least women only had one job to handle.

It's enough to give any modern-day woman a self-esteem problem. This section of the book, though, is not meant to defeat or deflate, but to help you understand that only a whole, healthy, happy woman can begin to work on making her marriage better. Even the most seemingly perfect women can use a little work in some area or another. No one is perfect.

Let's face it, women, we like to blame our marriage woes on our husbands. We say our marriages would be perfect if it weren't for our husbands. Do any of these phrases sound familiar? "If my husband would get a better job . . . If my husband wouldn't yell at me so much . . . If my husband would say he loves me every once in a while . . . If my husband would remember my birthday even one time . . . If . . . then our marriage would be perfect."

Let me submit that if you begin to work on yourself, your marriage may not be perfect, but you will look at it in a totally different way. You will begin to see that you have some issues to work on as well. Once you begin to work on yourself, then and only then, can you proceed with ideas to express your love to your husband.

A
Work on Yourself

Don't always blame everybody else. Work on yourself whether that means building up your mind, dealing with your emotions, or getting in better shape physically. Try enhancing those things that first attracted him to you. Do you know what those were? Ask him.

B
Pray On Spiritual Armor

Daily "pray on" the spiritual armor as outlined in Ephesians 6:10–18. Pray for yourself and your husband, saying, "Lord, thank you for dressing us with your helmet of salvation. Thanks for the sword of the Spirit, which is the Word of God; the belt of truth; the breastplate of righteousness; the shield of faith to extinguish the fiery darts of Satan and 'good news' boots to wear so we may share the good news with those who need to hear."

C
Get Close to God

In your deep relationship with God, you will find complete fulfillment. Nothing (your husband, job or family) will bring the contentment that a close relationship with your heavenly Father will bring. Regardless of what happens, your fulfillment is from God.

D
Learn to Let God Provide the Love You Need

God longs to love you and provide the love you need. His love is complete, eternal and unfailing. He says He will be your husband. Allow Him to fulfill all your needs. Your husband can be an earthly representative of the Lord and can be doing his best to be God's servant here on earth, but he will fail. He is human. If you rely on the Lord for your total fulfillment as a person, you will not be upset, controlling, angry or bitter when your husband fails to be all you need. If he is the most wonderful husband in the world and does everything perfectly, you will be blessed with a double portion of love. But expect him to miss the mark every once in a while. That's all right. You can forgive him. After all, you miss the mark sometimes too. Be complete within yourself, receiving God's unconditional love, and then the love you do receive from your husband will be an unexpected pleasure.

E
Pray for Yourself

Pray that you will become the kind of woman God wants you to be. Pray that you will have godly influence on everyone you meet. Pray that the inward qualities from 1 Peter 3:1–6 would be evidenced in your life. Pray that your husband would, as the husband of the Proverbs 31 woman, "rise up and call you blessed." (See Appendix D at the back of this book.)

F
Develop Spiritual Maturity

Seek to "fall in love" with Jesus Christ. Some women are afraid to develop themselves spiritually because they're afraid they will be more "spiritual" than their husbands. God may deal with you differently because you are married, but He still deals with you individually. You are responsible before Him to be the best daughter of God you can be. As you grow closer to God, you may find your husband will draw closer as well. If not, make it a part of your daily prayer time to pray for his spiritual growth. Don't expect your husband to grow at the same rate as you do. Work on your own holiness, not his. Don't judge his holiness. As you draw closer to God, He will reveal more godly ways for you to respond to your husband.

G
Allow God to Heal You

Allow God to heal your past hurts and fears. If you are dealing with an abusive past, seek God's advice through His Word about forgiveness. If you are still having difficulty, see a good Christian counselor; seek advice from godly teachers, especially women who have been through similar situations; read Christian books and listen to Christian tapes on the topic. (See Appendix I.) Actively seek to let go of the pain and tragedies of the past. Strive to make changes. You cannot change anyone else. You can change only yourself. And sometimes that makes all the difference.

H
Count Your Blessings

Make a list of all the blessings you have. Include the basics, such as home, car, job, family, material possessions, friends and church. List as many as you can. Then begin to think what life would be like if you didn't, for instance, have a place to live. That one-bedroom apartment may look much better after you have contemplated having no place at all. Your minimum-wage job may look much better than no job. Learn to be thankful for what you have, and do the best with what God has given you. If you have a small place to live, make it the best small place you can. Paint the walls, dress up the windows, dye materials to match or make throw pillows. There is a lot you can do to spruce up a home, even if you don't have much money. Take care of what you have been given. Change the oil regularly in your vehicle even if it is ten years old. If you are faithful with little, God may allow you to be steward over much.

I
Desire Inward Beauty

Seek a gentle and quiet spirit. Read God's Word daily. Spend quiet time alone with God. Find a time to do this, even if it means getting up at 3:00 A.M. and then going back to bed for a few hours. Find a quiet place daily to renew and refresh your spirit with God. Without that, inward beauty will be impossible.

J
Enhance Your Natural Qualities

What qualities attracted your husband to you in the first place? Was it your gentle spirit, your sharp mind, your perky personality, your ability to listen, your caring nature, your love of people, your ability to share deeply with others or your kindness? If some of these qualities have become buried through the years, dust them off and bring them out again.

K
Realize Love Is a Decision

You cannot make decisions on feelings. Feelings or no feelings, love is a decision. Love is a mental commitment, a decision we make to love and respect our husbands. When the flame seems to have gone out, realize the real "heat" is in the embers. (See Appendix G.)

L
Seek Counseling

When you are having problems in your marriage, you seek counseling even if he doesn't want it. Many times a professional counselor or the counsel or advice of a minister can help you deal with problems from your own perspective. Put aside your pride and find out what an expert has to say. Be teachable.

M
Put Mistakes behind You

Don't continually bring up his or your past mistakes. Guard your heart and his. Some mistakes can be humorous, but talk about his mistakes only if he brings them up. Learn from your own mistakes, and bring them up only if you can laugh about them and help someone else learn from them.

N
Trust

Learn to trust him, with decisions, with finances, with what he said he'd do and even with taking care of the baby! Tell him you trust him, then take your hands off.

O
Desire Harmony

One of the definitions of *submit* is "to harmonize." When you harmonize, you submit to another person in order for your voices to sound good together. One person, though, has to sing lead, while the other sings the supportive harmony. Sometimes the lead may be sung by the soprano, and sometimes it is sung by the baritone. It all depends on what song is being sung at the time. One may be stronger than the other, but in harmony, both blend to form one. Harmony should be the goal of a godly marriage.

P
Submit Your Moods to God

The old saying, "When Momma ain't happy, ain't nobody happy," is really true. The woman sets the tone of the home environment. Her mood can make or break a happy home. If you are unhappy, it permeates the entire family. Submit your moods to God. Take time out to get it right with Him.

Q
Be Content

Let go of worry. Worry breeds discontentment. In whatever state you are in, be content (see Phil. 4:12). It's important in your marriage to be content with your husband, your finances, your home, your car and so forth. You can have goals and dreams, but by being content, you relieve a lot of unnecessary stress on yourself and your marriage. You can't change anything by worrying, but you can add years to your life and your marriage by being content.

R
Maintain Your Own Identity

Yes, when a man and woman marry, they become one. But a woman also must be herself. Your husband was attracted to you as an individual before you were married. You must maintain your own identity, independence and confidence to be a whole person in your relationship.

S
Don't Expect Perfection

There are no perfect people, no perfect marriages. What you see as an imperfection may be a God-given trait and not an imperfection at all. After all, God used and still uses many imperfect people to accomplish His kingdom's work. And don't expect perfection from yourself. Let go of that superwoman image. Learn to say "no" to clients, social invitations and church work if it demands too much time away from your marriage and family. Learn to be yourself.

T
Read Good Materials
Fill your reading time with God's Word, Christian self-help books or Christian novels. Keeping your mind pure will help to keep your heart pure, which will help keep your home pure.

U
Make Prayer and Bible Study a Daily Habit
Set aside time each day for prayer and Bible study. You can read the Bible through in a year simply by dividing the number of pages in your Bible by the number of days in a year. Four or five pages a day is all it takes. Remember to listen to God's Spirit as you read. Keep a quiet-time journal. Some like to do this on the computer. Others use spiral-bound notebooks, three-ring binders or books designed for this purpose. The point is to keep a record of what you read in God's Word, what it says to you, what you want to do in response to the Word, your confessions, your praises and your prayer requests. If you are not doing this, begin now. You will be amazed to look back at your prayers a few years later and see how God has answered. You'll also be encouraged by what God has taught you.

V
Accept What You Cannot Change
Ask God to help you accept things you cannot change about your husband. Pray for his shortcomings and the things you think need to be changed, without trying to force the change. Be open to having God change your mind and attitude about your husband. Ask God to give you insight into yourself and your husband so you can understand why he is the way he is. Express your thankfulness to God for the things that you cannot change.

W
Have Your Own Hobbies

Hobbies provide relaxation and stress relief. You may enjoy any variety of hobbies on your own. Just make sure you don't put your hobbies before your husband, children, home and other duties. Hobbies can be relaxing, but they can also become addicting. Keep them in perspective, and they will help you become a more well-rounded individual.

X
Accept Criticism

When your husband says you need to do or not do something, what is your first response? Defensiveness? Accepting criticism is never easy or fun, but it can be highly beneficial. Even if you think the comments are undeserved, swallow and say, "Thank you for sharing your opinion. I'll think about it." Then pray and ponder over his remarks. Search for the element of truth in what was said. Accept the truth, and reject all else, including your own hurt and anger.

Y
Thou Shalt Not Nag

"Better to live on the corner of the roof than share a house with a nagging wife" (Prov. 25:24). "A nagging wife is like a constant dripping on a rainy day" (Prov. 27:15–16). Even when he forgets for several weeks to fix something that needs to be fixed, do not nag. You are his wife, not his mother. He is an adult. Be patient.

Z
Thou Shalt Not Whine

Don't whine about your problems or how much better others have it. A whiner is only concerned with herself—not with others. Have an accountability partner to talk to in confidence. Make sure it is a woman who will ask about how you are responding to your husband and who will encourage you to change your attitude and make amends when you are wrong. You can be her accountability partner as well.

CHAPTER ONE

Create and Continually Enhance Meaning and Value for Him

A s women we sometimes spend so much time cooking, cleaning, washing, ironing and grocery shopping that we forget there are other aspects to a marriage relationship. It is important to keep our husband's wants and needs in the forefront of our minds. How can we create meaning and value for him each and every day? What can we do continually to make sure he knows he is loved and appreciated?

Sometimes we are good at doing these things only once in a while. You might say, "Well, one time I told him I loved him," or "Last year, we prayed together when Sally was in the emergency room." But what are you doing each day that says you're a team, you're together and you rely on and appreciate him? Here are a few suggestions.

1
Pray Together Often

Praying together develops an emotional and spiritual bond that can span the difficulties of life. It forms a strong spiritual bond that God honors, but it also develops your relationship on an emotional level so that each of you knows the other more intimately. If there is a specific area of concern, pray about it when he mentions it. This gives perspective and encouragement. Do this even if one of you is a relatively new Christian and finds prayer uncomfortable. Don't use this time to preach or to ridicule the other's spirituality. A good starting point is to pray together at meal times. But quickly move beyond just saying grace.

Pray together about difficult decisions. Pray together when a crisis hits. Pray together for your children. Pray together about finances. Pray together for relatives and friends.

2
Don't Make Him a God

God says, "You shall have no other gods before me" (Exod. 20:3). He includes husbands in that category. It's easy for a wife to put her husband on a pedestal and make him into a god. When your husband doesn't perform in a godlike fashion, he falls from your pedestal, and both people are miserable. See him as he is, a unique son of the heavenly Father. He may be a great guy, but he is not a god. When treated like gods, many men run the other way. They know they can't possibly live up to that standard. Allow him to be human. By the same token, don't expect him to live up to a godlike standard you have set for him. Challenge him to grow spiritually, but accept him where he's at, also.

3
Read the Bible Together

Read the Bible together as a family at least weekly. Discuss the meaning of the passage and how it applies to you. Seek to understand and get to know each other better through reading God's Word. Find passages to claim for your marriage, your family and your ministry. Stand together on God's Word. Go to God's Word for answers to specific situations or problems. Seek to live according to God's Word. But don't use God's Word to win arguments or to get your way. Don't allow this time to be a substitute for your personal Bible reading and spiritual growth.

4
Love Your Husband

This should be a given. However, some women have no idea how to love their husbands. Read 1 Corinthians 13 to learn about real love. Instead of the word *love*, substitute, "My love for (_____ ____) is patient. My love for (_____) is kind. My love for (_____) keeps no records of wrongs. My love for (_____) never fails." Continue through the entire chapter. (See Appendix D.)

5
Don't Be Critical
Don't constantly be critical of your husband. Try not to criticize him in front of others. Don't question him in an attacking way. This is a common courtesy that many times we extend to everyone else except our mates. If you disagree with something he said or did, try talking about it in private instead of airing your "dirty laundry" in public. In the car after a party or at home later is the time to talk about things you disapprove of, not in the middle of a dinner party.

6
Never Go to Bed Angry
Never let the sun go down on your anger. Stay up all night if you have to, but don't go to sleep angry. Don't withhold your physical presence from him because of your anger.

7
Tell Him First
Never let him hear from someone else that something significant happened to you (or is about to happen to you). Don't tell his co-workers or yours, the folks at church or your family or friends before you tell him. Always tell him directly, even if you have to call him at work to let him know.

8
Restate What You Heard Him Tell You
People talk on different levels. Our husbands may be talking about something, and we get the idea they are directing a statement to us, when in reality they are just stating a fact. People use words differently. Some of us are better at expressing ourselves than are others. What he means to say may not be what we thought he said. For

instance, if your husband says, "I had a terrible day at work today. Why did I ever take this job anyway?" You might say, "Are you saying you want to change jobs or you're looking for a different job?" To which he might answer, "No, I think this is the best job for me; it's just that this was a killer of a day. Maybe I need to take some time off." If you assume he means he wants to change jobs, you may start scouring the want ads and asking friends about openings in their company, when he really didn't mean that at all. Don't assume you know what he means. Restate what you heard him say, and give him time to answer or correct what you said.

9
Encourage Humor

Clip cartoons, remember a good joke and tell it, laugh at his jokes, tell funny things your children said or did, watch a funny movie or television show, and laugh at yourself. Be willing to share your humorous side. Don't put him down if he shares his humor.

10
Don't Be Afraid of the Complete Truth

Jesus said, "The truth will set you free" (John 8:32*b*). The complete truth may be difficult to own up to at times, but it is always the way to freedom. Don't leave out parts or embellish to make yourself look better. Don't be afraid to tell your husband the truth, even if it means you have done something you wish you hadn't. Ask for his forgiveness.

11
Create a Marriage Covenant

Put into writing, individually and together, what kind of marriage you want and what kind of spouse you want to be. Decide what mission you desire for your marriage and what you hope it will accomplish in your lives, the lives of your family, your community and the world. Begin to see your marriage as more than just something for you; rather, see it as a testimony to what God can do with two people totally committed to Him. (See Appendix G.)

12
Make Homecoming Enjoyable

Greet your husband with a smile and a kiss. Let him know you are glad he is home just because of who he is and not because the sink is clogged and the oven stopped working and the dog is loose. If you arrive home after your husband, find him and tell him how glad you are to be home. Ask about his day, and tell him about yours before you get involved with your next chore or activity.

13
Make Family Times a Priority

Love, honor and cherish your family. Make family times together a priority. Schedule them if you have to, but make sure you have time together as a family. Take family trips and vacations even if they are just to visit relatives during a holiday.

14
Invite Him to Your Family's Activities

Invite him to events that involve your family, but allow him to decide not to attend if he doesn't want to go. Make sure he knows he is welcome, but don't take it personally if he decides not to attend. Forcing him to attend will end in disaster.

15
Show Value for the People He Values

Learn the names of his friends, their spouse's names, their occupations and so forth. Be interested in them and ask about them.

16
Develop Couple Friends

Develop friends you both enjoy. This can be another couple with children of similar age to yours. If you don't have children, you may want to develop friendships with other childless couples who have interests similar to yours.

17
Discover His Favorites

Make a list of "favorites" that you want to know about him. (Use Appendix E.) Give the list to him to fill out. Then try to memorize five new things each week about him. Use these for gift ideas or in conversation.

18
Remember His Likes

Don't decorate your bedroom in pink if he hates pink. Remember he has to sleep there too. Consider his likes when decorating the house, buying a car, going on a trip, planning a meal, picking a restaurant, going to the movies and choosing furniture.

19
Let Him Know Where You Are

Let him know where you are and where you are going to be. Call if you're going to be late. It's just as important to him to know you're safe, as it is for you to know that he is safe.

20
Begin Your Own Family Album

Start your own family photo albums of outings, homes and towns you have lived in, places you have visited, birthdays and other family events. Go through these and remember the good times.

21
Discourage Close Female Friendships

Discourage your husband from forming or maintaining close friendships with other females, especially with women you don't know. Other women can sometimes have impure motives toward your husband. Even if the woman's motives are pure and the relationship starts out innocently, it can end with temptation, sin and sorrow. Talk to your husband about the dangers of these kinds of relationships. Be firm about the fact that he should not spend time alone with any women.

22
Viva la Difference

Learn the emotional differences between men and women. Actively seek to discuss the differences as they apply to your marriage. (See resources listed in Appendix I.)

23
Dream Together

Dream a little. Think about some things that you would really like to accomplish. What would you like to accomplish spiritually, emotionally, mentally, physically or financially? When you're dreaming, the sky's the limit.

24
Let Him Know You Care

Why not do things to let him know you care? Send flowers to him at the office or his workplace. Include a sexy note. Send him balloons. Send a card to his office, or hide a card in his suitcase when he goes out of town. Put a "Welcome Home" sign on the garage even if he was just gone to work that day.

25
There's More to Life Than Things

If gathering material possessions is a major goal, it may force both of you to work harder. It may mean time away from each other and from your family. Work toward things that have eternal value, such as your relationship with your husband and family.

26
Set Goals

Take some of the more realistic dreams and set goals together to achieve those dreams. Goals should have projected finish dates, or they are still only dreams. Set some short-term, mid-range and long-term goals. It's easier for the two of you to cut back on spending if your agreed-upon goal is something you both want, such as a bigger home or completing an education.

27
Celebrate His Birthday

Make his birthday special. Ask him how he would like to celebrate his birthday. Don't assume he wants to celebrate it like you would like to celebrate yours. If he can't come up with any suggestions, ask him what his favorite birthday has been and try to improve on that. If he comes from an environment where birthdays were not celebrated and he doesn't have any ideas about how he would like to celebrate, then take into consideration the things he enjoys doing and come up with a creative celebration. If he enjoys being with one or two other people, plan a small meaningful dinner at a local restaurant. If he has three close male friends, then invite them and their wives or dates for cake, ice cream and a game of cards. If he enjoys being the center of attention, throw a big bash.

CHAPTER TWO

Encourage, Affirm and Support Him with Your Words

It's not a large part of the body, but it sure gets us in trouble more than we'd like to admit. Yes, I'm talking about that always-moving part—the mouth. Just as we can do much damage with the words we speak in haste and in gossip, we can also do much good. Our words can encourage, affirm and support our husband. Our words can praise our husband and lift him to a higher level.

Our words can encourage a new business venture, or they can present caution and concern when that is due. Our gently delivered words of correction can save embarrassment in public later. Our open admiration of our husband can help lift his self-esteem and confidence.

Let us be known as women who respect our husband's decisions even when others tell us he is wrong, even when we ourselves know he is wrong. Let us be women who are our husband's cheerleaders through thick and thin, in prosperity and adversity.

With our words, we can literally bring life or death to our husband. Nothing stings a man harder than the angry, biting words of a nagging, spiteful wife. The Bible says it is better to live on the corner of a rooftop than with a woman like that. So if you've been wondering why your husband is spending more time away from home, or when he's at home, why he's not around you, perhaps you should examine your words. Perhaps you should find ways to turn the dagger of your mouth into a weapon to protect your marriage, rather than kill it.

28
Praise Him through Your Words

Tell your husband what qualities you admire in him. When he helps a neighbor kid fix his bicycle, tell him you appreciate his love and concern for others and that he is using his spiritual gift of helps. Use your words often to let him know how you feel. Don't assume that he knows. Plan what you are going to say. Sometimes it's as difficult to use our words to praise someone as it is to tell someone something we don't like. But the more often you do it, the easier and more automatic it will become. Start today. (See Appendix C for suggestions.)

29
Complete, Don't Compete

Let your words complete your husband and not compete with him. It's easy to fall into the trap of always wanting to be one up on anyone, especially the person you live with. Work as a team. See him as a part of you. You wouldn't want to bad-mouth yourself, so don't do that to your husband.

30
Pray for Your Husband

This is the most important ingredient in a marriage. Pray for him daily. Pray that God would give him wisdom, strength, knowledge and power to overcome temptation. Pray for areas where he needs help and guidance. Pray for areas where you and he disagree, and ask that God reveal His plan to both of you. Your heavenly Father should be the only One to whom you reveal your specific displeasure with your husband, your anger over his faults and your desire to see changes in his life. Ask your husband for specific requests, so he knows you are praying for situations during the day. Find scriptures that apply to him or his needs, and use the Word to pray for him. Scripture prayers are powerful. Tell him you are praying for him. Encourage him with anything positive God reveals to you about him.

31
Respect Him

Do you respect your husband? If you respect him, others will respect him. Why was the husband of the Proverbs 31 woman so well respected when he sat at the gate with the elders? In part, probably because his wife respected him. (See Proverbs 31 in Appendix D.) Learn what respect means, and practice it.

32
Lies Don't Have Color

There is no such thing as a "white" lie. Eventually every dishonesty will come back to haunt you. Better to tell the truth the first time rather than try to cover it up. Covering it up only makes it worse. Honesty is the best policy.

33
Say "Please" and "Thank You"

Ask by saying "please," instead of demanding. You may not feel like you are demanding, but stop to think. To which of the following remarks would you rather respond: "Take out the garbage" or "Please take out the garbage"? Learn how and when to say thank you.

34
Be Honest about Your Past

Let your husband know what happened in your past. Be honest. If it is truly in the past, it shouldn't matter. Wouldn't it be worse if he found out from someone else? Make sure he knows more about you than anyone else. Develop your husband's trust by not allowing yourself to be put in situations that could compromise you or cause suspicion.

35
Write a List of Why You Love Him

Try to list at least 25 reasons why you love him. (See Appendix A for ideas.) Let these be spontaneous, not labored over. Let them flow from your heart. Do this even if writing is difficult for you. If he knows it was difficult, it will be more meaningful. Then share the list with your husband. Try being creative; for example, write them on the underside of the toilet seat, maybe with lipstick.

36
Do Things That Are Important to Him

Make a list of specific things you know are important to your husband. Plan to do one thing a week from your list. Decide which one you will do this week.

37
Leave Unexpected Notes

Finding love notes tucked away, even if they are as simple as "I love you and miss you," means a lot. Try tucking a few in various places, and see how long it takes for him to find them.

38
Learn How to Deal with Conflict

Every relationship has conflict. How you deal with conflict determines the level of agitation present in your household. Bring up things or situations that bother you right away. Don't let them fester. Avoid using words or phrases, such as "you always" or "you never." Try using phrases, such as "I feel . . ."

39
Praise Him through Writing

Write down the qualities you admire in your husband. Then send written notes that praise some of those specific qualities. Tape a note to the bathroom mirror, leave one on his desk at work or tape one to the front seat of his car. Try praising one quality at a time.

40
Call to Say "I Love You"

Call him to tell him you love him and are thinking about him and can't wait to see him. Keep the call brief and don't do it every day. But every now and then, give him that special call.

41
Say "I'm sorry"

Don't be afraid to admit that you made a mistake. Say "I'm sorry" to your husband and your children. Also say, "I was wrong. I made a mistake. Will you forgive me? I love you." Every man, woman and child needs to do this every day.

42
Forgive

When he does something that really hurts you, forgive him. Forgive him before he asks for forgiveness. Be quick to forgive. Keep short accounts. If you cannot forgive, ask God to help you. Your standing before God is contingent upon your forgiving others, especially your husband. Don't let the sun go down on your anger either. Love unconditionally and forgive continuously.

43
Ask for His Forgiveness

A teachable spirit is imperative in a godly relationship. When you do things that offend your husband, ask his forgiveness. Stop right now and ask God to show you anything you have done that you have not asked your husband's forgiveness for. Write these down. Then go to him with a humble attitude, and ask his forgiveness. Use the words, "Honey, please forgive me for . . ."

44
Tell Him What You Need

If you need to be held, let him know. If you need him not to give advice but to listen, tell him so. If you need him to try to understand what you're feeling, tell him so. Once you've told him or written it down for him, forget it. Don't continually bring it up. Encourage him to tell you what he needs as well.

45
Share Your Feelings

Share your feelings using "I" statements and illustrations. "I feel like a rose that had all its petals all fall off." "I" statements don't provide pressure for the individual listening. Encourage your husband to share with you, too.

46
Be Gentle but Honest with Him
Be gentle but honest, especially about the clothes he wears. If something doesn't match, is outdated or soiled and needs to be changed, tell him in a gentle but loving way. He'll thank you for the embarrassment it might save him later.

47
It's All Right to Disagree
If you disagree, that's all right. You will not always agree on everything. Make sure you each understand that you are individuals and have a right to your own opinions. If certain areas cause major disagreements, learn how either to compromise in these areas or to avoid discussing them if they are opinions that don't have much bearing on your relationship. It's OK to think differently, act differently and be different.

48
Allow Him to Be Himself
Don't assume your husband is going to be spiritually just like your father or just like your perfect perception of a husband. He is going to make mistakes. Allow him to make mistakes. We are all sinners saved by grace. Don't get angry. Comfort him. Get up and go on.

49
Affirm Your Husband's Maleness
Go to his sports events, and cheer for him. Go duck hunting with your husband, even if you don't want to carry a gun. Watch a football or basketball game with him. Participate in a hobby event with him. Admire your husband when he does what he is best at.

50
Develop Curiosity
Become curious about him, rather than judgmental. What does he do that is interesting? Don't judge it; investigate it.

51
Don't Force Him to Be the Leader
If your husband does not take the spiritual leadership in the family, don't force him. Don't be confrontational with him. Respect his feelings. Listen to what he feels and says.

52
Appreciate His Work
Tell him you appreciate how he works hard for you and your family. Many men and women go to work every day, come home and do it all over again. Let him know you noticed and you appreciate what he does.

53
Praise Him to His Children
Praise your husband to his children. Tell them how hard he works and what a good provider he is. Tell them how important he is to you and what a good husband and father he is. Children will tell their daddy what others say about him. If it is good, it will build up your relationship.

54
Support Him in Front of the Children
Whether or not you agree with his position or decisions, support him. Then talk about the differences in private. If you think he has punished too harshly or not harshly enough, support him in front of the children. If you come to an agreement different from what was said to the children, go to them and say you have talked about the situation and this is our decision. Don't be afraid to admit to the children you made a mistake.

55
Praise Him to His Coworkers
Say positive things about him when you are around his coworkers or boss. If they are prone to saying cutting or sarcastic comments, think of something positive to say in response. Don't agree with their remarks, even if they are meant to be humorous.

56
Praise Him to "the Guys"

Say positive things about your husband to his male friends and their wives. Make it a habit never to say negative things about him to others. Wives can make or break their husband's reputation in the church and community by the way they talk about their husband.

57
Correct with Respect in Public

His self-esteem is completely lost when you contradict him in front of others. Some women contradict their husband constantly. If this is your problem, try building him up instead. You can correct an error, such as a wrong date for an event, wrong address or directions. But do it in a manner that doesn't cast disparagement on your husband. Correct him with respect, especially in public.

58
Support Him in Public

When in public, support your husband. Even if he makes a mistake, support him as the strong man he is. You don't have to agree with him to support him. If he makes a fool of himself, he would probably like to know that there's at least one person who supports him and believes in him, even if he did blow it completely.

59
If His Peers Criticize Him, Don't Agree!

If your husband comes home from work and tells you of criticism he received from a boss or coworkers, don't agree with them, even if there is some truth to their criticism. Affirm him by pointing out his positive qualities. Talk with him, and try to get him to figure out why they might have said what they did. Encourage him to talk with them to understand their point of view.

60
Praise Him to Others

Tell others about your husband's great qualities and accomplishments. You can do this in front of him or when he is not present. Either way, it is praising him, and eventually it will come back to him. Build him up to others.

61
Be Open with Him

If he asks your opinion, tell him your true feelings. If these feelings are negative, you may want to wait until you are alone to let him know how you feel. If you're in public and he asks your opinion, simply say, "Let's discuss this later." If you have an opinion that is controversial, let him know what it is. Be open with him, even if you can't be open with others. Note: There is a difference between being open and being critical.

62
Share Your Honest Feelings

If your husband asks how you feel about any situation or decision, share your honest feelings. Even if you know your feeling needs to be changed, share honestly in a respectful way. Most husbands can't read minds. They need you to share with them, but often they're afraid to ask for your input because they think you might get angry.

63
Bear One Another's Burdens

When you know your spouse is weak in a certain area, help him by bearing that burden. If your spouse is weak in the financial area, design a plan to help him. You might write out bills together, and set a budget together. Find ways to help each other bear the burdens.

64
Do Unto Others . . .

"Do to others what you would have them do to you" (Matt. 7:12*b*, NIV). Jesus' advice is for wives and husbands, too. Do you want him to support you emotionally? Then support him.

65
Compliment His Efforts to Be Sensitive

If he made a special attempt to understand, listen or comfort you, let him know a day or several days later what he did that you particularly liked. He needs to be sensitive as much as you need his sensitivity. Calling attention to his efforts will feed both your needs.

66
Be Cautious of Others' Influence

If your husband works in an environment where other men and/or women are constantly separating from their spouses, divorcing, re-marrying or engaging in adulterous affairs, remember he is working under this influence day after day. Pray continually against harmful influences. Point out to him that these influences are present, and although you love and respect him and know that he loves you, these kinds of influences cannot help but affect him. Ask him to pray continually for strength and to be on his guard. Pray together for the people your husband works with. Pray about the situations you find yourselves in, and proactively plan how to make wise choices in future situations.

67
Compliment His Repair Efforts

When he fixes the front door, changes the oil in the car, hangs a picture or repairs a leaky faucet, tell him you appreciate his help. Even if he can't complete the project himself, tell him you're glad he made the effort.

68
Build Him Up to His Family

Don't tell his mother or his family about his bad habits. Tell his family about the positive things he does. If they say negative things to you about him, respond with the flip side. Be his cheerleader.

69
If You Can't Say Anything Nice, Don't Say Anything at All

Don't use sarcastic humor at your husband's expense. Never joke about your husband's physical qualities, personality traits or emotional or spiritual maturity. Your jokes might get a few laughs, and others might even do it and not harm his self-esteem, but it sheds a totally different light on things when *you* joke about your husband. Grandma's rule applies here, "If you can't say anything nice, don't say anything at all."

70
Pray for Him Instead of Manipulating Him
Don't trick or manipulate him into anything. Be specific with your requests. If he says no or if he says he needs to think about it, don't dream up ways to get him to do what you want. Pray for him and for the specific situation, asking God to show both of you the right answer. Realize you could be the one whose opinion or expectations need to change.

71
Let Him Be in Control
Allow him the freedom of being himself and making his own decisions. Don't try to control everything in his life. Home should be a place of freedom, not a prison or a place of drudgery. Allow him time to relax. Don't schedule his every minute or suggest things he should be doing if he needs to relax.

72
Watch Your Tongue
Encourage your husband with your words. "Don't return insult for insult" (1 Pet. 2:6–7). Remember, your tongue can either cut him down or build him up. If he cuts you down or yells at you, don't fall into the trap of cutting him down or yelling at him in return. Even if you are angry at what he has said, exercise self-control. Words spoken in the heat of the battle are often regretted. That doesn't mean you shouldn't confront him later about the way he talked to you if he was out of control. If you watch your tongue, you won't have to apologize for rash words. Once spoken, words—good or bad—can't be taken back.

73
Speak Only Positive Things

Gossip is such an easy trap to fall into. For some reason, most women think their husband wants to hear the gossip they've heard. In reality, most men would rather not hear gossip. So don't repeat gossip to anyone, especially your husband. Don't gossip about your husband or his past to your friends. Don't gossip about his friends either. This can kill a relationship quickly.

CHAPTER THREE

Spend Time with Him

Families today live such fast-paced lives. Between children and jobs and demands at home, no one has time for anything. Who has time for themselves, much less time to relax with another person? But if our marriages are to last, we must schedule time alone with our mates. It doesn't have to be a long period, but it must be time just for him. The television, that great killer of family time, must be turned off. The newspaper must be laid aside. The bookmark must be put in the new novel. We must even stop folding the laundry for a few minutes, while we listen and give attention to our mates.

To spend time with your husband, you may both need to agree on how much time you need and how often. Do you need 10 minutes a day when he gets home to spend together without any distractions? Do you need a night out once a week? Do you need a weekend away once a month? Do you need a week together once a year? What does each of you need? Discuss it, and try to plan it. Make it a priority, if it is a priority to him.

74
Know Him Face to Face

Learn to know each other face-to-face. Look into his eyes during private, intimate times. Watch his face, his expressions. Touch his face, his eyebrows, his ears and his lips. This is the most intimate way of looking at another person.

75
Celebrate Your Differences
You look differently, act differently and relate differently. You probably have different spiritual needs, desires and goals. Your spiritual natures complement each other like other areas of your life complement each other. Celebrate and relish your differences. It would be a dull world if we all were alike.

76
Give Him Eye Contact
When your husband is talking, give him eye contact. Listen to what he is saying. Stop watching television and watch him. Stop reading your book and look at him. Put down the newspaper or magazine. It will improve your understanding of what he is saying and will let him know he matters to you.

77
Couch Time
Give him undivided attention at least 15 minutes a day. Some call this "couch time." It might be when he first comes home from work and you sit down at the kitchen table and talk things over. It might be after the kids have gone to bed and you take some time to talk. It might be just before or after you turn out the lights each evening. Find a time that works for you and give him your undivided attention and ask for his as well. Don't pay bills, mend or paint your fingernails. Look into his eyes and ask about his day, and then listen to what he says and how he feels. Don't try to solve his problems; just let him know you hear him and understand.

78
Listen
The art of listening is a lost art. Learn to listen to your husband without reacting negatively to what he is saying. Repeat back what you thought you heard him say: "It sounds like you feel . . ." Then draw him out by asking, "Do you also feel . . . ?" Follow the advice in James 2:19: "Be quick to hear, slow to speak and slow to anger."

79
Enjoy Your Husband

Focus on his positive traits, and enjoy being with him. When negative things come up, deal with them and move on. Always keep in mind his most fetching characteristics. "Till death do us part" is a long time. Enjoy each other while you can.

80
Understand Your Husband's Personality

There are many good books on personality traits. Understanding the strengths and weaknesses of your husband's personality type and yours will help you work together in harmony. You can compensate for his weaknesses rather than clashing with them. And he, yours. (See Appendix I for books that might be helpful.)

81
Acknowledge His Position

You may not understand his position or agree with him about everything, but you can immediately acknowledge his position and his right to have that position. "I know you are the head of our home, and I want to support you. But I thought I heard you say . . ." Then ask him to clarify your understanding. You have a right to your own opinion, even if it is different than his.

82
Speak in Normal Voice Tones

Don't scream or yell when you are talking to your husband or your children. Screaming and yelling doesn't get the job done faster; it usually drives a deeper wedge between you and the person you are screaming at. Like the moral of "The Boy Who Cried Wolf" story, yelling should be reserved for times when a person is in real physical danger.

83
Respond to Your Husband's Praise

When your husband praises you, let him know it makes you feel good. Simply say, "Thank you." Show by your smile and cheerful expression that what he said made a difference to you.

84
Crown Him "King for a Day"

Celebrate your husband as "King for a Day." Let him do what he wants for the day. It might involve going away for the day together, providing him with a fantasy night, renting a limousine and taking him out for dinner or renting a hot-air balloon and taking a ride together. Put together a scrapbook about his life, and present it to him on this day. If you really want to go all out, have a *This Is Your Life* presentation for a few friends. Put together slides or movies of his life. Tell about who he was as a child and who he is now. Praise his virtues to his friends and family.

85
Confess Your Faults to Each Other

Confess your weaknesses to each other, and ask your mate to pray for you in the areas you are struggling in. Confession requires trust that your mate will not use what you share against you. It is not easy to bare one's soul to another. It's much easier to be physically intimate than emotionally intimate. Just like in a share group, you'll never get beyond news, weather and sports unless someone makes the first move to share on a deeper level. You may have to make the first move in confessing your faults, but you will be demonstrating your trust in your husband.

86
Plan an Activity Just for Him

Plan a special activity just for him. Plan a weekend for the two of you filled with activities he enjoys. Let him know it is his weekend and he gets to do whatever he likes.

87
Talk about the "What Ifs"

After you've been married for a while, you may feel like you've run out of things to talk about. Try asking "what if" questions. This is especially good to do if you are traveling in the car together and have lots of time. Talk about things, such as these: "What if someone gave you lots of money and told you to spend it helping people. How would you spend it?" Or "What if you could spend a day with any five people who have ever lived; whom would you choose?" Or "What if you could wave a magic wand and change one thing about yourself, what would it be?" If you're really brave, you can ask what he would change about you. But don't ask unless you really want to know.

88
Allow Him to Cry
Many men don't like to be seen when and if they cry. Many women don't know what to do if a man cries. Let him know it's all right with you if he needs to cry and that tears are a sign of maturity, not weakness. Hold him without talking. Be near if he doesn't want you to hold him.

89
Teach by Example
If you want to be held during a difficult time, hold him during a time that's difficult for him. If you like it when he asks about you, and you sense he's upset or having an off day, ask him how he's feeling or if everything is all right. Ask him what he needs. Learn to comfort him in the way he desires to be comforted.

90
Add Variety
Routine can become boring. Add variety to your lives by reading books and magazines. Have something new and interesting to talk about. Try something you've never done before, and treat it as an adventure.

91
Remember His Important Dates
Remember dates that are important to him. If the date he graduated from high school and the annual meeting of Hobbyists International are important to him, mark them down.

92
Exercise Together

Find time to exercise together, whether it's walking, running, bicycling or doing aerobics, exercising will keep you both in better shape and will reduce stress, fatigue, listlessness and irritability.

93
Attend a Spiritual-Gifts Retreat

It will help each of you to know your own spiritual gifts, your passions and those of your mate. You may choose to take a "Network" course, attend a spiritual-gifts retreat or read a book on spiritual gifts. Encourage your husband when you see him using his spiritual gifts. (See Appendix I.)

94
Discover Your Ministry as a Couple

Ask God to reveal what ministry opportunity He has for you as a couple. Make its fulfillment a priority. Look at many of the successful couples in ministry you know. They have discovered how their gifts as individuals can complement each other. One wife is a minister and teacher, while her husband is the administrator and handles the finances. One partner is the outgoing, talkative type, while the spouse is the serious, contemplative sort. Together they make a great counseling team. Find what works for you. Couples may teach Sunday school together, with one doing the research and study, and the other spouse adding the teaching tools that bring the information alive for the students. Try helping newlywed couples. While the husband is doing a Bible study with the men, the wife can be doing practical classes for the women and vice versa. The exciting thing is to discover how your gifts can work together. (See Appendix I for resources to help in this discovery process.)

95
Find a Common Activity to Do Together

Select some activities you both enjoy. If you don't have activities you do together, sit down and discuss some things you might like to try.

If you're too busy to add another thing, perhaps some things you both do should be eliminated to make room for some together times.

96
Learn from Him

Let your husband teach you something new. Maybe he has a hobby you don't understand, or perhaps he knows about geography and you know don't. Allow him to teach you. Let him lead in this. Be interested and involved in what he is saying and teaching.

97
Play at the Park

Go to a local park and play together. Swing, run, throw a Frisbee, have a picnic, fly a kite, feed the ducks, watch the squirrels or sit and talk on a park bench.

98
Go on a Nature Walk

You may not enjoy hiking in the woods. That's all right. Try shorter walks first. If taking a walk in nature seems akin to torture, try to find ways to enjoy it. Watch for the uniqueness of God's creation. Stop and enjoy a spider spinning a web or a squirrel gathering nuts.

99
Know about the Sports He Plays

Does he enjoy golfing, bowling and softball? Whatever sports he plays, you should know the basics or be willing to allow him to teach you the basics. Read about the sport. Learn what you can. If you can, learn to play the sport so you can participate together. You may think golfing is boring, but you'll never know until you try it. Be happy for him that he really enjoys doing something active. Get joy and satisfaction from it because he gets joy and satisfaction from it. Allow him to watch or participate in sports without hassling him about it.

100
Play Board Games Together

Choose games you both enjoy, not for competition but for pleasure. You might try some of the old favorites such as Monopoly, Scrabble or Yahtzee. Involve your children or just play alone. Put on your favorite Christian tape and enjoy the time together.

101
Know about His Hobbies

Does your husband enjoy railroad memorabilia? Does he like to garden? Whatever his hobbies, show an interest in them and learn what you can about them. You may find that you share a common interest or that you can become interested in it yourself.

102
Plan a Date Night

Set a date night once a week or once a month. Make it a time just for the two of you. The place is not as important as the time you set aside for each other.

103
Have a Lunch Date

Meet him for lunch at a restaurant, for a walk in the park or for lunch at home just the two of you. Make it a date, and stick to it as a priority. Put it on your calendar. Make it the last thing to be canceled, not the first.

104
Allow Him to Tell the Truth

Our reaction to the truth may make our mates never want to be truthful with us again. Allow him to tell you the truth, without getting angry or being shocked. Practice being calm in the face of difficulty. Show interested concern, not censure. If he's made a mistake, the last person he needs badgering him is you. Remember you are his wife, his companion, his mate and his soul-partner, not his mother. If he made a mistake, he has to own up to it and reap the consequences. Support his truthfulness. Figure out the solution to the problem together.

105
Watch a Sunset Together
Take time at the end of the day to watch the sun set and enjoy the beauty God has created in the skies. It can be a time to reflect on the day or to enjoy silence together.

106
Take Weekend Trips
Take occasional weekend trips if long vacations are too expensive. Leave the children at home or with a sitter so you have time to rekindle the flame.

107
Do a Missions-Related Activity
Go on a missions trip together. It can be an afternoon spent helping build a Habitat for Humanity house or a weeklong trip in another country. Have fun helping others together.

108
Know about His Job
Do you know what your husband does for a living? Could you explain it to someone else? If he is an insurance agent, know about the various kinds of insurance. You don't have to be an expert, but understand it enough to converse with his peers.

109
Read a Book Together
Find a topic you both enjoy, and read a book about it together. Take turns reading aloud while the other person does a repetitive task, such as driving or painting. Try making chapter assignments and dates to discuss what you've read. Ask his opinion on the issues or the characters. If you choose a novel, don't give away the ending—unless he begs.

110
Watch a Romantic Movie

Watch a romantic movie together. Hold hands like you did when you were dating. Imagine your husband as the leading man and yourself as the leading lady.

111
Go Camping

Camping provides a sense of togetherness that no other activity provides. Yes, there may be some difficult times, such as rain or wind, but there will be some memorable times, enjoying God's beautiful creation. Later you'll reflect on the hard times and how you pulled through together.

112
Spend Weekly Family Time

If you have trouble being together as a family, make one night a week a family night to do something together. Or just make sure you do something together as a family at least once a week. Make it a point to go with your husband and children when they decide to go for a walk, ride bicycles or go for a car ride.

113
Rediscover Him

Who is this man you are married to? What are his likes and dislikes? What is his favorite color? What's his favorite time of the year? What dress of yours is his favorite? Find out all you can about him. Go on a mission to rediscover your mate. (See Appendix E for ideas.)

CHAPTER FOUR

Serve Him in the Home

Servanthood has gotten a bad reputation. It's all right to serve another person out of a heart of love. If the other person takes advantage of you and requires you to serve them or forces you to serve them, that is another thing. But service to anyone is a godly principle.

The Bible tells us that Jesus Himself is our example of serving others.

> Do nothing out of selfish ambition or vain conceit, but in humility consider others better than yourselves. Each of you should look not only to your own interests but also the interests of others. Your attitude should be the same as that of Christ Jesus. Who, being in very nature God, did not consider equality with God something to be grasped, but made himself nothing taking the very nature of a servant, being made in human likeness. (Phil. 2:3–7)

If Jesus can do it, so can we. You remember the story of Jesus washing the disciple's feet. He didn't have to do that. He did it out of love and service. He did it as an example to us. Why is it easier for us to think about washing a friend's feet than washing our husband's feet? Maybe we should start at home. Maybe we should wash our husband's feet. What would he think if he came home from work, hot and tired, and sat down in his favorite chair to read the newspaper and his wife removed his shoes and socks and washed his feet in warm, soothing water? Try it one day and see.

Here are some other suggestions. If you're not one to serve, don't try all these at once. If you are more prone to service, try changing your attitude to one of joy rather than drudgery, or pick a service-oriented task that relates specifically to your husband, one that he will know you are doing just for him.

114
Serve with Gladness
Mop, clean the oven, clean out the refrigerator, sweep, dust and pick up clutter with a song. Enjoy the privilege of serving your family.

115
Organize Your Home
Organize your home so that the space is utilized to its best advantage. Clean out closets, rearrange pantry shelves or rearrange children's drawers and closets. Do a major organizational reworking often. Don't do this without talking to your husband about it. Be organized, but don't be so rigid you can't have fun.

116
Set the Home Environment
Play Christian music. Choose Christian radio or television programs. Have Christian videos available for your children. Hum a Christian song. Sing a Christian song while you're working around the house. Pray out loud as you work. Display Christian pictures or scriptures in attractive ways. Make your home a place of comfort. Let it be a place where he feels welcome and honored. Pray for God's peace to be in your home.

117
Make Sure He Gets Enough Food and Rest
Food and sleep are essential to any individual. Many men are especially hard to live with if they don't have enough sleep or if they are hungry. Let him sleep late on his day off, or allow him to take a nap when he gets home from work. Keep supper warm and waiting when he gets up from his nap.

118
Cook His Favorite Meal

Cook his favorite meal for a special occasion or "just because." Let him know you're cooking it just for him. If it's something the children don't like, let them learn to like it or eat peanut butter sandwiches. Let them know this is Daddy's night and complaining is not allowed.

119
Spice Up Your Meals

Take a cooking class or try a new recipe from a magazine or new cookbook. Having the same food can become routine and boring. Try something new, even if it doesn't work.

120
Make a Budget

Make a budget, and stick to it. There are some great resources available to help you plan a budget (See Appendix I). Basically, you need to start by writing down everything you spend for several months. Then, categorize the expenditures to see how much you are spending for food, clothes, housing, car expenses, insurance, recreation, savings, investments and so forth. Finally, set a budget you can live with to accomplish the goals you both have. Take advantage of the expertise of those who help families set up budgets. Ask your pastor to refer you to someone.

121
Put His Needs First

Your husband's needs are more important than getting to that meeting on time, whether it is a physical, emotional or spiritual need. Don't let activities rule your life. Make the marriage and your relationship with your husband a priority.

122
Be Flexible

Even though you have a schedule, be flexible enough to set aside some time to listen to your husband unwind after his day, to take a walk with him or to spend the day at a hobby fair when you were planning to do laundry. Setting aside your agenda to pay special attention to your husband will deepen his affection for you.

123
Yield

Learn to yield to your husband on matters that do not violate your own conscience and are not of prime importance in the great scheme of things. Does it really matter if he buys a new garden hose or not?

124
Allow Him to Lead

If your husband understands his position as the spiritual leader, allow him to lead. Ask his advice. Listen to what he has to say. God will bless him with spiritual insight as the spiritual head of the family. When someone asks a spiritual question, wait for him to answer. Don't automatically jump in with your answer. Allow him to lead whether you agree or not. This will be difficult if you have a history of bad relationships or if your husband doesn't like the leadership position. Start with little things. Try asking his advice regarding whether or not you should teach a specific lesson to your Sunday-school class, if you should have made a comment during Bible study or if you should take on a specific job at church. If he gives advice, try following through with what he said. As God leads, begin to take his advice regarding larger matters. However, don't assume you know what he would say. Take a minute to discuss it with him. You'll be amazed at the insight God will give your husband when he is acting in his God-given role as head of the household.

125
Agree on Major Decisions

Agree never to make final decisions that affect both of you and/or the family unless you agree. Take time to hear each other's viewpoints on the situation or matter and understand the position each of you has before making the decision. If you disagree, wait. Pray about the decision, and wait some more. If you still can't agree, explore a com-

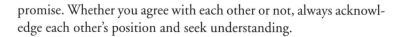

promise. Whether you agree with each other or not, always acknowledge each other's position and seek understanding.

126
Decide on Giving

Decide together what, when, and how much you will give to church and charity. If your husband doesn't agree with tithing or giving, agree with him on what portion of the income is considered yours so that you can tithe or give from your portion. If he agrees with the principles of tithing and giving, have fun deciding how much you can give and plan ways to give more. It's true: You can't outgive God.

127
Keep a Family Calendar

Keep a master family calendar. On it write down events, such as family get-togethers; doctor appointments; children's school and sports events; meetings like church care groups and other activities, and keep it in a place where everyone can find it.

128
Have a Place for His Clothes

Don't assume that because you have more clothes, you need a bigger closet. His clothing is just as important as yours is. Perhaps you should take some of your clothes out of the closet and store them. You can only wear so much at one time. Make sure he has adequate dresser space. Don't relegate him to one drawer and the back corner of the closet.

129
Help Him Look His Best

Iron his shirts or put them back in the dryer to fluff out the wrinkles. Suggest what type of clothes to wear to different events. Encourage him by telling him which colors make him look best.

130
Clean House Together

With many men and women both working outside the home, time is at a premium. If you share the cleaning, you will have more time to do other activities together. Set aside a time to get the house cleaning done. Agree on chores for each of you.

131
Make Sure the House Is Clean

Even a man who doesn't mind clutter, enjoys coming home to a clean environment. It may not be a top priority on your list, but it should be on the list. If you don't have time to clean it yourself, here are some ideas. Pay your children to clean it. Barter with a friend in exchange for watching her children or performing a professional task for her. Pay a friend who needs extra money, or pay a cleaning service to clean. As one woman said, "It's cheaper than a marriage counselor."

132
Make a Chore List

Yes, it's true. Men love *and* hate these kinds of lists. But why not make a list of chores and divide them evenly and age-appropriately among all the family members. Agree on a time to do the chores or a time by which the chores should be done. Include your own chores on the list. Let your family see that doing house chores is a family responsibility. Then plan a special reward (such as a special meal, a night out, a movie night, etc.) after all the chores are done.

133
Agree on Spending

Most men make more than their wives, but in some cases it is the other way around. Agree on how money is going to be spent and how much each spouse may spend for "fun." Don't hassle over the way he spends his "fun" money.

134
Know Your Finances

If your husband takes care of the finances, make every effort to understand them. Know where your checking and savings accounts are and what investments, annuities and insurances you have. It would be a good idea to have these written down and put in a safe-deposit box or other secure location.

135
Share Financial Responsibility
Regardless of who pays the bills, finances should be a shared responsibility. Both of you should know where you stand on payments, bills and debts.

136
Keep Track of His Relatives' Birthdays
Help him keep track of his parents birthdays and birthdays of brothers, sisters, aunts, uncles, grandparents or others in the family. Even if his family doesn't celebrate birthdays, everyone still enjoys a card on their birthday. Keep track of his parents' anniversary, including the year. Write them on a family calendar, along with other special family events.

137
Keep the Kids out of His "Stuff"
Honor his wishes, his space and his possessions. By doing this, you are supporting him and allowing him to be the head of the home. Teach your children to honor his wishes as well.

138
Design Your Dream Home
Design the home of your dreams together. Ask him what he would like if he could have anything he wanted in a home. Begin a dream-home notebook. Clip pictures from magazines. Save scraps of fabric. Write down ideas. Who knows? One day you may have that dream home.

139
Serve Him as Your King
Try serving your husband one day a week as if he were your king. Give him the royal treatment, and let him know that it is his day. Try to anticipate his needs. Bring him his paper, cup of coffee and breakfast in the morning. Offer him the recliner, TV remote, slippers and cold

soda when he gets home from work. Make his favorite dinner. Pray for him at the dinner table in front of the children. Listen to his ideas and the things that happened that day. Don't ask him to do any chores for you. When he's ready for bed, run a hot bath for him. Dry him off and give him a massage. Remember this is his day, so let him decide the direction for the rest of the evening. Perhaps he wants to go to bed early and get a good night's rest. Or maybe he has something else on his mind. Be available to please him in any way he desires.

CHAPTER FIVE

Physically Adore, Honor and Love Him

Let's face it, physical attraction of some sort is probably what drew you and your husband together in the first place. Physical touch is part of that attraction, and although it doesn't always have to lead to sexual intercourse, it is nonetheless, an expression of how you care for your husband.

Anything you can do to make your sexual experience more enjoyable for both of you will only enhance and deepen your relationship. Set aside time for your husband. Go to bed early with him. Lounge in the bedroom with him. Enjoy his company before and after lovemaking. Contrary to popular opinion, he wants more from you than just sexual intercourse. You are his wife. He wants and needs to know that you care about him and love him. Show your feelings by your gentle and loving touch.

140
Know His Physical Needs

A man is constructed differently from a woman and has different desires, wants and needs. A man has a physical need for sexual release. There may be times when you are not in the mood to make love, but your husband has a physical need. Be aware of his need and let him know what you need in order to help him. One woman described it as having a "snack" every once in a while, waiting for the "full-course banquet" another time.

141
Learn to Hug

Hug your husband intimately. Snuggle up close to him. Wrap your arms around him and let him know you mean it. Allow every part of you to touch every part of him.

142
Hold Hands

Hold hands while you're walking together, in church singing or praying, standing together or sitting together. Allow it to be natural to hold hands with your husband.

143
Praise His Physical Ability

Praise his virility and his physical ability. Let him know he is the most desirable man around to you. See him in all his manly beauty.

144
Compliment His Appearance

Women receive compliments on their appearance all the time. Very few men receive compliments on their physique. Find things to compliment about your husband: his muscular arms, his chest, the color of his eyes, his smile, his firm handshake. Let him know when he's chosen clothing that looks good.

145
Touch Him

Touch him as you set down his cup of coffee, as you walk past him, as he's sitting in the living room chair, when you come over to him in a room full of people, as you are praying together at church or at other times. Touching him often is a way of connecting with him.

146
Be Gentle

Men need the gentle touch of a woman. They need to hear a woman's soft voice. Don't feel as if you have to treat him as one of the guys, slugging him in the arm and slapping him on the back. It was your difference that attracted him to you in the beginning. Try touching him all over before touching him in a more intimate way. Let your fingers touch him lightly and gently. Let him indulge in being gently touched by you. Caress his muscles; run your fingers down his arms, his legs, along his back and over his chest. Trace his eyebrows and his face. Enjoy every part of him. He is a unique and wonderful creation of God.

147
Remember the First Time You Made Love with Him

As the years go by, you learn how to please your mate and sex becomes more and more enjoyable. It's pleasant sometimes to remember the first few times you made love and how you have progressed in your experience. If your first time was better than your current time with him, think about what you can do to make your current time as exciting or as exhilarating as the first.

148
Plan Time Alone after Being Apart

If you know he is going to be gone for several days, plan to spend time alone with him when he returns. Build it into both of your schedules. Make sure children are taken care of and your time will not be interrupted. Make it an intimate time of talking, as well as touching and lovemaking.

149
Cuddle with Him

Cuddle with him in front of the television or in front of a fireplace. Cuddle with him before you go to sleep at night without expecting sex. Cuddle with him after sex to let him know just being with him is important. Wrap yourselves around each other for at least five minutes before and after making love. Try to spend more time if you can.

150
Give Him a Massage

Use powder or lotion and rub his back and neck. Pay attention to muscles that are tense. Massage his feet and legs. Watch out if he is ticklish. The focus should be on helping him relax.

151
Initiate Intimacy

It's all right for you to initiate making love. It might seem unnatural to you, but it is good for your relationship and your intimacy if he knows you desire him too. A woman needs to be emotionally, mentally and spiritually prepared to engage in lovemaking. By letting your husband know you are ready, you will both feel more satisfied.

152
Let Him Initiate Intimacy

If you have been the one to initiate lovemaking most of the time in your marriage, stop. Let your husband be the initiator. Let him know you still care for him and love him, but tell him you want to please him by waiting for him to be the initiator. Then wait. Most of the time, you won't have to wait too long. Allow him to ask if he may make love to you. Respond positively when he does.

153
Slow Down

Allow your lovemaking to blossom and unfold like a beautiful flower. Don't rush the experience. Although men many times are guilty of this, women can be the guilty party as well. Take time with your husband. Try to make your time together last as long as possible. If you normally take 15 minutes, try stretching it to 30 minutes, then more. How about an hour or two? Be creative in making your time together last as long as possible.

154
Be Inventive

Encourage intimacy in different locations rather than just the bedroom. Suggest to him that you try outside under the stars, in a different room in the house, in the car. Encourage intimacy at different times of the day. Be inventive.

155
Allow Him to Please You

Allow your husband the pleasure of pleasing you. Give up control of yourself to him. Allow yourself to get lost in the pleasures he is providing. Don't feel guilty about enjoying yourself and letting go.

156
Tell Him How Wonderful You Feel

A man has no idea how a woman feels during lovemaking. Tell him during and afterward how wonderful he makes you feel. During times when you have been especially satisfied, let him know. Don't assume that he knows. Tell him with your words. It builds his self-confidence and bonds you together.

157
Set the Mood

Setting the mood for intimacy will help in your sexual relationship. Change the sheets on the bed, and make it as attractive as possible. Lower the lights or use candlelight. Have soft music playing. The bedroom should be the most inviting room in your home.

158
Draw a Hot Bath for Him

Draw a hot bath for him when he's tired and needs to relax. Add bubbles or soothing bath oil. If he's willing, crawl in with him and enjoy touching and washing him. If not, just sit and talk with him while he's relaxing. Taking a shower together also can be fun.

159
Kiss Him

Kiss him passionately. Don't be afraid to allow his kiss to linger. Find reasons to kiss him. Kiss him when he leaves. Kiss him when he comes home at night. Kiss him when he fixes the stopped drain. Kiss him when he takes out the garbage. Kiss him when he disciplines the children. Kiss him when he's down. Kiss him before you go to sleep. Kiss him, especially, when you're making love.

160
Wear His Favorite Negligee

Wear his favorite negligee, or meet him at the door (of your bedroom), wearing nothing but his favorite perfume. Throw out those old nightshirts with holes in them or nightgowns that are threadbare.

161
Be Playful

Making love should be fun, not a somber, serious time. Encourage playfulness during the day, as well as during lovemaking.

162
Leave the Lights On

What you do with your husband is something God created. It doesn't have to be done in the dark. It can be done in the light. Focus on your husband while you are making love.

163
Let Lovemaking Be Spiritual

Making love should be an experience that involves every part of you. Pray that God will be the third party in your sexual experience. You can pray together, or you can pray silently and individually at the beginning of making love. Ask God to reveal to you special ways to please your husband. After all, He created him. He knows better than anyone does, how your husband's body works. Making love with your husband can be spiritual warfare because it is communication at the very deepest level between a man, woman and God. Many times, Satan will try to drive a wedge between a husband and wife at this level. If he accomplishes that, he breaks the unique union between husband and wife. Satan does not want husbands and wives to enjoy each other. He is in the business of thwarting relationships rather than aiding their unity. If you are having trouble enjoying this time with your husband, commit it to prayer. Ask God to help you enjoy physical intimacy with your man. Pray after making love. Pray aloud. Thank God for your husband and all his special qualities. Be specific.

164
Say "Yes" More Than "No"

An old adage says, "Never refuse your husband." It's the advice of mothers to daughters on their wedding day. Although it sounds good, it's not practical. It is practical to say "yes" much more than "no." "No" should be reserved for times when you are physically, emotionally and mentally exhausted. Even when you're tired, though, you can take a few minutes to satisfy your husband, even if you are not personally satisfied. "No" should always be followed by the specific reason and a suggested time when you can say "yes."

165
Take Care of Yourself

Take care of yourself physically. If having sex is physically painful, see a doctor. If there is no physical problem, see a counselor. Sex is not the only part of marriage, but it is an important part. Don't let a problem go for a long time before talking to a professional. And talk to your husband about it too. Your husband may love you a lot, but he can't read your mind. If you are refusing sex because it hurts, you need to let him know. There may be a very simple solution to your problem, or it may be more involved. Whatever it is, find a way to solve it so you can enjoy this wonderful and exciting gift of God.

166
Men Have Different Needs

Remind yourself that men usually need sex more often and more regularly than women do. Make love to him more often than just when you need it. Learn to give love to him as a special gift.

CHAPTER SIX

Give Him Gifts of Love, Time and Concern

Some men don't feel loved unless they receive frequent gifts from their wives. If your man is one of these, find ways to give a variety of gifts. Gifts don't always have to be bought. Some gifts can be made. Others can be gifts that involve your time and concern.

Even if your husband doesn't need gifts to feel loved, giving him gifts can help him understand that you do love and care about him. If you need to limit your spending, give things that don't cost money. Let him know that you are giving him a gift of a free day to do whatever he wants, or give him the gift of taking out the garbage when it's usually his job.

A word of caution: Husbands who are overly concerned with finances and don't want their wives to spend money on items that aren't budgeted, will not appreciate a gift, especially if it is a costly item. You may be trying to express your love, but he may see it as just the opposite. This type of husband enjoys receiving a gift that doesn't cost money.

For other husbands who relish the thought of receiving gifts, larger amounts of money spent won't matter. As a matter of fact, if you do not work outside the home, you may want to ask for an amount each month for purchasing gifts. (Include birthdays for children and relatives in this budgeted amount.) If he enjoys receiving gifts, he will see this as a necessary expense.

167
Make Lists of Wants and Needs

Each of you should make a list of at least five wants and needs you would like your mate to do, excluding sexual activities and touching, to show love to you. The lists should not include don'ts. Swap lists. You pick things from his list to do. Try to do at least one thing each day. His list might read: "Clean off the kitchen cabinet. Make the bed. Open the blinds to let light in. Talk in a normal voice to the children. Put the mail on the bureau." So every day when you make the bed, he will take that as a tangible sign of your love for him. When he does things from your list, thank him, smile and show appreciation. The purpose is not to find out which person does more tangible activities, but to be aware of things you do out of love.

168
Respect His Space

Every person in the family needs space to call their own, especially your husband. If he has a hobby, make sure he has somewhere to build things and store equipment and tools.

169
Attend a Marriage Workshop

Encourage him to attend a marriage workshop with you. Or watch a Christian video series on marriage. Read books on marriage. (Appendix I lists several books.) Take personality tests to help you better understand each other. (See Appendix I.)

170
Let Him Get Away for a Few Days

Help him arrange time to get away by himself for a couple of days to focus on God's desires for his life and for your family. He might want to combine it with a trip related to a hobby, such as a convention or show. Just allow him to be away from you for a few days of reflection without any demands on his time except those he sets. Some men may choose time alone at a lake cabin; others might want a golfing weekend.

171
Tell Him You Love Him in Fun, Creative Ways

Buy him candy and write a note, incorporating the name of the candy bar into some special message. For example, buy him a bag of Hershey's Hugs. Include a note that says, "I love your hugs." Or be creative and buy him a bunch of nuts and bolts with a note that says, "I'm nuts about you." (For more ideas, see Appendix B.)

172
Send Him a Letter

Send him a letter or note that answers the following: "I appreciate you because . . . I admire you for your . . . Thank you for . . . I feel confident that you can . . . You made me feel loved when . . . I like being with you because . . . You're the best I know at . . . ."

173
Buy Him Clothing Necessities

Ask if he wants you to purchase clothing necessities like underwear, socks, jeans and shirts. Be sure you're giving him equal attention in this area. Don't buy clothes for yourself and the children but not for him. Include him on the list as well.

174
Buy Him Gifts

When you see that special item you know he'd like, even if it's just a left-handed screwdriver that costs $1.59, buy it for him. It's the thought that counts, not the amount.

175
Go through Family Photo Albums Together

Going through old family photo albums together provides great impetus for conversation about his childhood. Ask about the pictures: where he lived, what school was like then, what he was doing, where his parents were working and how they treated him.

176
Do Something Outlandish

Do something extravagant and outlandish. Fill the bed with rose petals. Fill his car with balloons. Send him 40 cards on his 40th birthday. Take out a full-page ad that says, "I Love You." Hire a skywriter to spell your love for him in the air. Literally, the sky and your pocketbook are the limit on this one! Here's a challenge: Find the most outlandish way to tell him you love him, while spending the least amount of money.

177
Show Gratitude for His Family

His family is responsible for bringing him into the world and raising him. Let them know you are grateful for what they did for him. Accept them and honor them, but don't try to be perfect—the model daughter-in-law. Be willing to spend time with them. When visiting them, agree ahead of time when you will leave, and ask your husband to initiate leaving. It's easier for parents to say good-bye if they realize their son is saying it's time to go rather than their daughter-in-law. Your husband will know what works best with his parents. Maybe they can take your suggestion of leaving easier than his. Whichever way works best, talk about it ahead of time.

178
Allow Him to Say "No"

If he wants to spend Saturday on a woodworking project instead of accompanying you on a trip to the mall, let him. Don't take it personally if he has something else he wants to do.

179
Allow Him to Be Quiet

Everyone needs quiet time. After a long day, your husband may need some time to reflect and be quiet. Don't force him to talk if he doesn't want to. By the way, you probably could use some quiet time too. You can be quiet together.

180
Know His Favorite Foods and Fix Them for Him

What are your husband's favorite foods? When does he enjoy eating them? If you don't know, ask him. Use Appendix E to list these foods and the way he likes them prepared. Then fix them for him on special evenings.

181
Study His Interests

If your husband is interested in airplanes, study about airplanes. Read what you can. Then drop little tidbits of information you've discovered into the conversation.

182
Allow Him to Spend Time with "the Guys"

It's important for your husband to have some male friends with whom he can talk and gain spiritual insight. An accountability group or Bible study is a healthy group in which to be involved. Be happy for him that he has male friends. You should have some female friends with whom to talk and spend time.

183
Give Him Time Alone

Sometimes your husband may need time to be home alone. If this is true, give it to him. Don't urge him to go to every event that you think is important. He may need some time to work on hobbies or take a walk. Ask him if he needs time alone, and then give him the gift of that time by taking the kids to the park or a movie. If you don't have children, go shopping or spend time with a friend so he may have the house to himself. Or allow him to be alone in his workshop or hobby area, while you read or do other things in another part of the house. Realize that this is not a rejection of you, but a need of his to be alone.

184
Remember Him

Remember him when you go to the discount store. You buy Johnny a new pair of jeans, Sally gets a new set of barrettes, you get panty hose and makeup, but what did you get him? Even if it's a pair of socks, remember him, too. At the grocery store, buy him a special treat that's just for him and no one else. Tell the kids that this is for Daddy. When they ask for some of Daddy's treat, tell them they have to ask his permission. If he's not home, tell them they have to wait until he gets home and ask him. Don't simply buy something everyone needs or likes and tell him it's his. Make sure it really is his.

185
List Things You Can Do to Show Love
Make a list of things you would be willing to do, including sexual activities and touching, to show your love for him. Show him your list and ask him to put a star beside the items he would appreciate your doing. Do your best to accomplish at least one of these things.

186
Surprise Him
Find ways to surprise him. Send flowers to his place of business. Mail a card to his office. Put a note on his windshield. Send the kids away for the evening, and surprise him with a night alone, complete with a candlelit bedroom. Pick him up at the office, and take him to the park for a walk and a picnic lunch.

187
Ask How You Can Improve
Ask your husband how you can improve at your God-given responsibility of being his wife and the mother of his children. When he gives you his honest answer, thank him. Write down the things he said to you and begin praying about how you can improve, asking God to show you what to change. Even if you don't see a need to change, pray about his request and ask God to help you understand and remember to do as your husband wishes. For example, you may not feel you need to call when you are going to be late coming home from work. But since he has asked you to do it, take a minute to call home. Don't expect to receive thanks or an acknowledgment from him if and when you do the things. Make the changes out of love and conviction that they need to be made, not for recognition.

188
Make a Tape of His Favorite Songs

Make a composite tape of his favorite songs, even if you hate those songs. Make the extra effort to beg or borrow CDs or tapes from which to copy a song or two. It may take some digging on your part to discover his favorite songs! (You can't resell this tape, but you can copy it for his pleasure.)

189
Show Kindness

Show kindness to your husband and your children. Would you treat an acquaintance the way you treat your husband and children? Would you be more likely to go out of your way for a friend or for your husband? "Be ye kind one to another" (Ref. ?:?) applies to husbands as well as strangers.

190
Write Notes When He's Gone

When he's packing for a business trip, write a note to him for each day he'll be gone. Put the notes in envelopes with instructions about when to open them. Write encouraging things. Tell him you are proud of him, you love him and you appreciate him. Include a scriptural encouragement. Remind him what pleasures will be waiting for him when he comes home.

191
Order Magazines

If your husband enjoys various hobbies, buy him magazine gift subscriptions about that hobby. Large bookstores usually sell specialty magazines. Ask the clerk to recommend a magazine in your husband's area of interest. Buy a sample magazine first. Then order a subscription if he expresses interest. Try reading the magazines yourself.

192
Plan Not to Annoy Him

Write down specific things you do that you know annoy your husband and ways or plans of action to deal with these problems.

CHAPTER SEVEN

Just Because You Love Him

There are things we do for our husband because we love him. These don't need any special reason. Some of them can be tough to do, but we do them because we love our husband and because we know it would be best for our marriage.

193
Let Him Go

Let him know you care, but don't smother him with your attention to the point that he feels he can never be alone. An old saying goes, "If you love someone or something, let it go. If it returns to you, your joy will be hundredfold."

194
Choose Sounding-Boards Carefully

There are times when a woman just needs to talk to another woman. Other women, if they are godly women, can be good sounding-boards to help you see areas where you need to improve. Be careful, though, whom you select. It should not be a church minister, church minister's wife, mutual friend, his relative or too close a friend to both of you. When talking to others, be careful to respect your husband's dignity.

195
Wear What He Likes

If your husband likes you to wear dresses, try to wear dresses every once in a while and let him know you're doing it for him.

196
Let Him Speak for Himself
Don't volunteer him for tasks at church, at a friend's house or at a relative's place. If someone calls and says, "Do you think your husband would do this or that," politely suggest that they ask him. Tell them when and where he can be reached. If you accept for him, then it's your responsibility to get him to do it. If he accepts for himself, the responsibility is his.

197
Know What It Takes to Achieve
Know what it takes to achieve prestige in his job, hobby or sport. If getting an extraclass amateur radio license is special, let him know you are proud of him. If getting a title change in his job is rare, even if it doesn't bring a monetary promotion, let him know you think it's great.

198
Don't Be Afraid to Do Things Alone
Don't be afraid to do things without your husband. Have you ever gone to a movie alone? Gone out to eat alone? Enjoyed an afternoon in the park alone? You need to learn how to enjoy yourself. If you don't enjoy you, how can anyone else enjoy you?

199
Help Him Be Cautious about the "Damsel in Distress"
Discourage his need to rescue the "damsel in distress." Encourage him to be cautious. Many times if a man offers to have his wife talk with a woman seeking his help, the woman suddenly doesn't need help. By offering to act as a first line of defense, you can help him weed out the truly needy from those who desire more than help.

200
Be Secure in Who You Are
Most women have something physical about themselves that they don't like. Don't continue to bring up the flaw, whatever it is. Ask God to help you see yourself as He sees you. Your positive feelings about yourself will provide a healthier physical relationship between you and your husband. If you like yourself, it's a lot easier for others to like you.

201
Use the Perfume He Likes

Men get used to the scent of their wives. Ask if he has a preference as to what perfume you wear, and then stick with that. It will help him know what to buy for you. Your special perfume will linger in his mind and in his heart.

202
Hand Over the TV Remote

If there is a discrepancy at your home over what to watch on television, hand over the remote to your husband. If it's a football game, he may not care if you watch it with him. But if it's a show that he enjoys and wants you to watch it with him, take the time out for his sake. Try to enjoy it. Television is much more temporary than we hope your marriage is.

203
Dedicate a Song to Him

Call up his favorite radio station or the one you know he'll be listening to (such as a station that is played at his workplace) and dedicate a song to him.

204
Make the Bed and Turn Down the Covers for Him

If you have something you need to work on and can't go to bed with him, take some time get the bed ready for him. Turn back the covers, and leave a love note and a mint on his pillow. Tell him in the note that you miss him already and that you'll be joining him soon. It'll make going to bed alone more enjoyable and the anticipation of your arrival that much more exciting.

205
Nominate Him for Something

Is there a contest for Husband of the Year, Best Father or Most Handsome Legs? Nominate your husband and give him a copy of the nomination form. He might not win, but it will help him know that you think highly enough of him to nominate him.

206
Plan a Rendezvous

Most everyone eats lunch or takes a lunch break. Why not invite your husband to a noon rendezvous at home. Have lunch ready and waiting (maybe even packed in a bag for eating on the way back to work) and the bed turned back for some middle of the day fun. It might be a quick rendezvous, but it is guaranteed to put the fun back in your marriage.

207
Love His Children

Love his children and parents because you love him so much. Find ways to show his family that you care. If you can't find a way to appreciate his parents, appreciate them because they gave him life and raised him. Appreciate his children because they are his flesh and blood.

208
Seek to Please Him

Tell him you want to please him in every way. Ask him how you can please him, how you can be his lover, how you can be his mate and companion. Listen to what he says and pick out at least one thing you can do to please him more.

209
Listen with Your Heart

Listen with your heart, not your head. Don't try to solve his problems. Be his soul mate. Empathize. Try to understand and feel what he is feeling.

210
Forgive

Learn to forgive. If you don't forgive, you will harbor much hurt that will eventually cause you emotional, mental and physical pain. Why not forgive now? Unforgiveness hurts you much more than it does the other person.

211
Be Supportive

Support your husband's opinions. Never side with your father and mother in an argument against your husband. Talk it over when you are alone. Give him your opinion only if he asks for it. Even then, don't make it sound like you are siding with them against him. If he is wrong, pray for him to change his mind.

212
Learn His Love Language

How does your husband like to receive love? Learn what he interprets as love, and pick out at least one thing each week to do to show him you love him, using his special language.

Appendix A ~ I Love You Because

I love you because you are you.
I love your gentleness.
I love your strength.
I love your humor.
I love the strong feel of your arms around me.
I love looking at you across a crowded room and knowing you are my husband.
I love your mind, the way the wheels turn and knowledge spills forth.
I love your creativity.
I love your playfulness, your boyishness and your ability to have fun.
I love your easygoing nature and your love of everything innocent.
I love the way you love me.
I love the way you take time to love me and be with me.
I love the way you hold me.
I love the feel of you beside me in the middle of the night.
I love the security of knowing you are here.
I love the way you provide for me and the kids and take care of us.
I love that you are committed to us.
I love that you stay and work things out rather than running at the first hint of discord.
I love that you are interested in many different things.
I love your soft, steel blue eyes.
I love your strong hands and muscular arms.
I love you because God created you, unique and special.
I love you because you are you and there is no one else like you.
I love you because you are the husband God gave me, and I am a whole, healthy, happy woman who delights in your love.

APPENDIX B - Inexpensive and Creative Gifts for Your Husband

Here are some inexpensive and creative gifts to purchase for your husband to tell him in special ways how much your relationship means.

- A balsa airplane with a note that says, "Come fly with me."
- A kite with a note that says, "You take me higher."
- An assortment of nuts and bolts with a note that says, "I'm nuts about you." The same note can be used with a can of peanuts, cashews or assorted nuts.
- A tape measure with a note that says, "There's no tape measure large enough to measure my love for you."
- A flashlight or a box of light bulbs with a note that says, "You light up my life."
- Some stick-up hooks for his closet or bath area with a note that says, "I'm hooked on you." You can use the same words when you buy your fisherman some new fishhooks.
- A bag of chocolate-covered pretzels called "Flips" and a note that says, "I've flipped for you."
- A calculator and a note that says, "How do I love you, let me count the ways."
- His favorite candy and a note that says, "I'm sweet on you."
- A garden shovel or another kind of shovel with a note that says, "I dig you."
- A roll of tape or a bottle of glue that he uses and a note that says, "I'm stuck on you."
- A puzzle and a note that says, "You make all the pieces of my life come together."

- A photo album or roll of film and a note that says, "Let's keep making memories."
- A watch with a note that says, "It's time I told you again, 'I love you.'"
- A box of Glad trash bags and a note that says, "I'm glad we're together."
- A CD or tape of one of his favorite songs or groups and a note that says, "You're like sweet music to my ears" or "Our love is a symphony."
- Fluorescent, stick-on ceiling stars and a note that says, "Our love was written in the stars." You could use this same note with a book about stars, a telescope or binoculars.
- Something to hide in his suitcase when he goes on a trip: a blue marker and a note that says, "I'm blue without you."
- Something else for his suitcase: a teddy bear with a ribbon around its neck and a tag that says, "I can't bear to be without you."

APPENDIX C ~ Words That Encourage

D o not let any unwholesome talk come out of your mouths, but only what is helpful for building others up according to their needs, that it may benefit those who listen" (Eph. 4:29). Here is a list of words you can use to build up your husband. Choose some to use now. Add some of your own. Mark all of those that apply to your husband. Note specific times you saw him display these traits. Begin to praise him when you see him displaying these traits.

Peaceful	Artistic
Powerful	Creative
Prayerful	Gifted
Loving	Intelligent
Caring	Flexible
Kind	Adventurous
Helpful	Inventive
Serving	Sympathetic
Respectful	Wise
Joyful	Prophetic
Patient	Supportive
Good	Adaptable
Self-controlled	Friendly
Gentle	Easygoing
Persistent	Carefree
Disciplined	Good natured
Skillful	Independent
Clever	Self-sufficient
Tactful	Loyal
Expert	Calm
Diplomatic	Casual

Trustworthy
Charming
Warm
Enthusiastic
Secure
Generous
Sociable
Decisive
Optimistic
Practical
Likeable
Capable
Important
Healthy
Happy
Cheerful
Competent
Muscular
Masculine
Contemporary
Handsome
Virile
Manly

Vibrant
Visionary
Tactful
Unselfish
Truthful
Honest
Energetic
Athletic
Rugged
Irresistible
Stable
Steady
Tough
Smart
Knowledgeable
Spiritual
Resourceful
Understanding
Emotional
Faithful
Concerned
Merciful
Imaginative

APPENDIX D ~ Scriptures

W rite your name and your husband's name in the appropriate places. Then read the scriptures out loud, and note areas you need to change in order to come in line with what the scriptures are saying. Several scriptures are listed here, but you may want to do this with other verses also.

1 CORINTHIANS 13: 1–8, 13

If _____ speaks in the tongues of men and of angels but has
  (Your name)
not love for_____ she is only a resounding gong or a clanging
   (Your husband's name)
cymbal. If_____has the gift of prophecy and can fathom all mys-
   (Your name)
teries and all knowledge and if_____has faith that can move
    (Your name)
mountains, but has not love, _____is nothing. If _____
    (Your name)   (Your name)
gives all she possesses to the poor and surrenders her body to the flames,
but has not love for_____, _____ gains nothing.
    (Your husband's name) (Your name)
_____ love for_____is patient._____love
(Your name) (Your husband's name) (Your name)
for_____is kind. _____love for_____does
(Your husband's name) (Your name) (Your husband's name)
not envy. _____ love for_____does not boast.
  (Your name) (Your husband's name)
_____love for_____is not proud. _____love
(Your name) (Your husband's name) (Your name)
for_____is not rude. _____love for_____
(Your husband's name) (Your name) (Your husband's name)
is not self-seeking. _____love for_____is not easily
  (Your name) (Your husband's name)
angered._____love for_____keeps no record of
  (Your name) (Your husband's name)
wrongs. _____love for_____does not delight in
  (Your name) (Your husband's name)
evil but rejoices with the truth. _____love for_____
   (Your name) (Your husband's name)
always protects, always trusts, always hopes, always perseveres.
_____ love for_____never fails.
(Your name) (Your husband's name)

And now these three remain: faith, hope and love. But the greatest of these is _____ love for _____.
(Your name)   (Your husband's name)

1 PETER 3:1–4

_____, in the same way be submissive to _____
(Your name)   (Your husband's name)
so that if he does not believe the Word, he may be won over without words by _____ behavior, when he sees the purity and reverence of _____ life. _____ beauty should not come from outward adornment, such as braided hair and the wearing of gold jewelry and fine clothes. Instead, it should be that of _____ inner self, the unfading beauty of a gentle and quiet spirit, which is of great worth in God's sight.

PROVERBS 31:10–31
(a paraphrase with personal goals)

A wife of noble character who can find? She is worth far more than rubies. _____ has full confidence in _____ and lacks nothing of value. _____ brings _____ good, not harm all the days of her life. _____ clothes her family by selecting quality clothing at reasonable prices. _____ is like the major grocery warehouse purchasers bringing her food from afar. _____ gets up while it is still dark; _____ provides food for her family and portions for her helpers. _____ considers property and buys it; out of her earnings she invests in commercial ventures to make additional income. _____ sets about her work vigorously; her arms are strong for her tasks. _____ sees that her trading is profitable, and she stays up into the night. She oversees the administration of her home and gives a hand when needed. _____ opens her arms to the poor and extends her hands to the needy. When it snows, she has no fear for her household; for all of them have boots, coats, gloves, hats and warm winter clothing. _____ makes coverings for her bed, making it a delightful place for _____; she makes sure she takes care of her body and sees that her clothing is of good quality and looks nice on her. _____ re-

spects _____ and _____ is respected when he meets
       (Your name)   (Your husband's name)
with his bosses and other important individuals. _____ works
                               (Your name)
at her home-based business and deals with other professionals.
_____ is clothed with integrity and can laugh at the days to
(Your name)
come. _____ speaks with wisdom, and faithful instruction is
     (Your name)
on her tongue, because she spends time with God and studies His
Word. _____ watches over the affairs of her household and does
      (Your name)
not eat the bread of idleness. _____ rise up and
                                  (Your children's names)
call her blessed; _____ also, and he praises her, "Many
             (Your husband's name)
women do noble things, but _____ surpasses them all." Charm
                        (Your name)
is deceptive, and beauty is fleeting; but _____, a woman who
                             (Your name)
fears the Lord, is to be praised. Give her the reward she has earned
and let her works bring her praise at the city gate.

EPHESIANS 5:21–33

Submit to one another out of reverence for Christ. _____,
                                       (Your name)
submit to _____ as to the Lord. For _____ is the head
      (Your husband's name)   (Your husband's name)
of _____ as Christ is the head of the church, his body of which
   (Your name)
he is the Savior. Now as the church submits to Christ, so also
_____ should submit to _____ in everything. However,
(Your name)   (Your husband's name)
_____ must love _____ as he loves himself and _____
(Your husband's name)   (Your name)   (Your name)
must respect _____.
         (Your husband's name)

APPENDIX E ~ List of Husband's Favorites

Birth date: _____

Shoe size: _____ Sock size: _____ Belt Size: _____

Pant size (Waist): _____ (Inseam): _____

Shirt size (Neck): _____ (Sleeve length): _____

Undershorts size: _____ Undershirt size: _____

Suit-coat size: _____ Overcoat size: _____

Hat size: _____ Glove size: _____ Eye color: _____

Favorite colognes:_____

Favorite shaving cream: _____

Favorite razor: _____ Favorite razor blades: _____

Favorite toothpaste: _____

Favorite mouthwash: _____

Favorite color: _____

Favorite food dishes: _____

Favorite meal: _____

Favorite desserts: _____

Favorite restaurants: _____

Favorite candy: _____

Favorite meat: _____

Favorite beverage:_____

Favorite soft drink: _____

Favorite juice: _____

Favorite ice cream: _____

Favorite doughnut: _____

Favorite pie: _____

Favorite kind of chips: _____

Favorite cookies: _____

Favorite fruit: _____

Favorite vegetable: _____

Favorite Kool-Aid® flavor: _____

Favorite hardware store: _____

Favorite "general" store: _____

Favorite holiday: _____

Favorite hobby: _____

Favorite tools and brand: _____

Favorite month: _____ Favorite day of the week: _____

Favorite year: _____ because _____

Favorite movie: _____

Favorite actress: _____ Favorite actor: _____

Favorite Bible person(s): _____

Favorite book in the Bible: _____

Favorite Bible verses: _____

Favorite relative: _____ Favorite in-law: _____

Favorite kind of pet: _____

Very most favorite person in the world and why? _____

_____

Favorite music singer: _____

Favorite song: _____

Favorite kind of music: _____ Favorite radio station: _____

Favorite vacation spot without kids: _____

Favorite vacation spot with kids: _____

Favorite camping spot: _____

Favorite friend: _____ Favorite coworker: _____

Favorite teacher: _____ Favorite grade in school: _____

People he considers to be heroes: _____

_____

Favorite name he likes to be called: _____

Favorite gift he ever received: _____

Favorite birthday party ever: _____

Favorite birthday gift ever: _____

Favorite book: _____

Favorite automobile: _____ Favorite motorcycle: _____

Favorite sport: _____ Favorite sports team: _____

Favorite sports person (current): _____ (past): _____

Favorite television program: _____ Favorite shape: _____

Additional items: _____

_____

APPENDIX F ~ Dos and Don'ts

Be his mate, not his counselor.
Be his cheerleader, not his judge.
Be his coworker, not his boss.
Be his light, not his burden.
Be his software, not his system error.
Be his coach, not his umpire.
Be his freedom, not his ball and chain.
Be his fire, not his water.
Be his hope, not his red flag.
Be his maiden, not his old hag.
Be his friend, not his mother.
Be his helper, not his slave driver.
Be his complement, not his competitor.
Be his Cinderella, not his wicked stepmother.
Say "Go, Honey," not "Stop, Stupid."
Be his rose, and he'll want to handle you gently.
Let him be the king, and you'll be his queen.

APPENDIX G ~ Marriage Covenant

When developing your Marriage Covenant, make sure it is your own statement. It can be copied from other documents, but make it is something you both believe. Here is a sample Marriage Covenant from a marriage of 20 years.

We promise to love, honor and respect each other, to support and uplift each other, trying always to encourage and never to discourage the other. We promise to be honest with one another in gentle and respectful ways, not to be sarcastic, cutting or angry.

We desire for our love to be modeled on biblical principles and to deem the other partner as more important than ourselves. We will strive to love each other unconditionally and to base our love on the example set forth in 1 Corinthians 13. We promise always to forgive each other as Christ forgave us. We promise to take care of each other in times of stress, sickness or injury. We promise to raise our children, living lives of godly example before them.

We desire for our marriage and home to be the foundation of ministry in whatever direction God takes us. We recognize there is an enemy who would desire that our marriage not be strong. We recognize anything that comes against our unity as being an attack of Satan and will covenant to pray, read the Bible, attend church and grow spiritually to keep the enemy out of our relationship.

Realizing that a three-strand chord is not easily broken, we covenant together with God to commit our lives to each other, realizing that love is a decision. We make the decision today and forever that we will love each other with the help of our heavenly Father who is able to keep everything committed to Him from this day forward.

APPENDIX H ~ *Additional Resources*

Many of these organizations hold marriage workshops:

Covenant Makers Marriage Workshops and Spiritual Gifts Retreats
P. O. Box 1882
Columbia, Missouri 65205
1-800-378-5085

Joyce Meyer @ Life in the Word
P.O. Box 655
Fenton, Missouri 63026
1-800-727-WORD

Gary Smalley @ Today's Family
1482 Lakeshore Drive
Branson, Missouri 65616
1-800-848-6329

Dennis and Barbara Rainey @ Family Life Marriage Conferences
(Affiliated with Campus Crusade for Christ)
P.O. Box 23840
Little Rock, Arkansas 72221-3840
1-800-FLTODAY

Dr. Gary and Barbara Rosberg @ America's Family Coaches
2540 106th St., Ste 101
Des Moines, Iowa 50322
1-888-767-2374

Dr. John Trent @ Encouraging Words
    12629 North Tatum, Suite 209
    Phoenix, Arizona 85032
    1-800-900-8640

Dr. James Dobson @ Focus on the Family
    Colorado Springs, Colorado 80995
    1-800-232-6459

Bishop T. D. Jakes @ The Potter's House
    P.O. Box 5390
    Dallas, Texas 75208
    1-800-BISHOP2

Relationship Resources, Inc.   (405) 789-2900

United Marriage Encounter   1-800-334-8920

National Campaign to Protect Marriage   (513) 733-8908

Marriage Watchers International   (303) 987-8583

[Publisher and date needed for all titles.]

APPENDIX I - *Book, Tape and Video Lists*

Books on Audiotape:

Bradshaw, John. *Creating Love.*
Gray, John. *Men Are from Mars, Women Are from Venus.*
Gray, John. *Mars and Venus in the Bedroom.*
Jakes, T. D. *Lord, Save Our House.*
Meyer, Joyce. *The Family Survival Kit.*
Smalley, Gary. *Hidden Keys to a Loving Relationship.*
Smalley, Gary. *Homes of Honor.*
Smalley, Gary. *Love Is a Decision.*
Smalley, Gary and John Trent, Ph.D. *The Blessing.*
Smalley, Gary. *Making Love Last Forever.*

Videotapes:

Jakes, T. D. *Marriage: Bonding or Binding.*
Jakes, T. D. *Give the Man What He Wants.*
Smalley, Gary. *Hidden Keys of a Loving, Lasting Marriage.*

Books:

Backus, William and Marie Chapian. *Telling Yourself the Truth.*
Barr, Debbie. *Children of Divorce.*
Beavers, Kenneth A., Ph.D. *Self-Worth without Self-Worship.*
Blackaby, Henry and Claude King. *Experiencing God.*
Blue, Ron and Judy. *A Woman's Guide to Financial Peace of Mind.*
Bolin, Cay and Cindy Trent. *How to Be Your Husband's Best Friend.*
Bugbee, Bruce, Don Cousins and Bill Hybels. *Network.*
Bugbee, Bruce, Don Cousins and Bill Hybels. *Network Participant's Guide.*
Burkett, Larry. *How to Manage Your Money Workbook.*
Buscaglia, Leo E., Ph.D. *Loving Each Other.*
Chapman, Gary. *The Five Love Languages.*

Chapman, Steve and Annie. *Married Lovers, Married Friends.*
Cole, Edwin Louis. *Communication, Sex and Money.*
Dobson, Dr. James. *Love for a Lifetime*
Dobson, Dr. James. *Love Must Be Tough.*
Farrar, Steve. *If I'm Not Tarzan and My Wife Isn't Jane, Then What Are We Doing in the Jungle?*
Ferguson, Dr. David, et al. *The Pursuit of Intimacy.*
Gray, John. *Men, Women and Relationships.*
Gray, John. *What You Can Feel, You Can Heal.*
Gruen, Ernest. *Touching the Heart of God.*
Harley, Williard F., Jr. *His Needs, Her Needs: Building an Affair-proof Marriage.*
Heald, Cynthia. *Becoming a Woman of Excellence.*
Heald, Cynthia. *Intimacy with God.*
Heald, Cynthia. *Loving Your Husband.*
Hocking, David and Carole. *Romantic Lovers: The Intimate Marriage.*
Honor Books. *God's Little Instruction Book on Love.*
Hunt, T. W. *The Doctrine of Prayer.*
Hunter, Brenda, Ph.D. *Home by Choice.*
Hybels, Bill. *Too Busy Not To Pray.*
Hybels, Bill and Lynne. *Fit to Be Tied: Making Marriage Last a Lifetime.*
Jakes, T. D. *Woman, Thou Art Loosed.*
Jampolsky, Gerald G. *Love Is Letting Go of Fear.*
Johnson, Greg and Mike Yorkey. *The Second Decade of Love.*
Kennedy, Nancy. *Help, I'm Being Intimated by the Proverbs 31 Woman.*
Kreidman, Ellen. *Light His Fire.*
LaHaye, Dr. Tim. *I Love You but, Why Are We So Different?*
Littauer, Florence. *Personality Plus.*
Markman, Howard, Scott Stanley and Susan L. Blumberg. *Fighting for Your Marriage.*
McCallum, Dennis and Gary DeLashmutt. *The Myth of Romance.*
McGee, Robert S. *The Search for Significance.*
McGinnis, Alan Loy. *The Friendship Factor.*
Minirth, Dr. Frank, et al. *Passages of Marriage.*

Moorehead, Dr. Bob. *Before You Throw in the Towel.*

Rainey, Dennis and Barbara. *Building Your Mate's Self-Esteem.*

Rosberg, Dr. Gary. *Do-It-Yourself Relationship Mender.*

Sell, Charles and Virginia. *Spiritual Intimacy for Couples.*

Sledge, Tim. *Making Peace with Your Past: Help for Adult Children of Dysfunctional Families.*

Smalley, Gary. *For Better or Best.*

Smalley, Gary. *Hidden Keys of a Loving, Lasting Marriage.*

Smalley, Gary. *How to Become Your Husband's Best Friend.*

Smalley, Gary. *Love Is a Decision.*

Smalley, Gary. *Making Love Last Forever.*

Smalley, Gary and John Trent, Ph.D. *The Blessing.*

Smalley, Gary and John Trent, Ph.D. *The Language of Love.*

Smalley, Gary and John Trent, Ph.D. *The Two Sides of Love.*

Sprinkle, Patricia H. *Women Who Do Too Much.*

Swindoll, Charles R. *Strike the Original Match.*

Stoop, David. *Experiencing God Together.*

Talley, Jim, Ph.D. *Reconcilable Differences: Healing for Troubled Marriages.*

Tannen, Deborah, Ph.D. *You Just Don't Understand.*

Tannen, Deborah, Ph.D. *That's Not What I Meant!*

Tirabassi, Becky. *Being a Wild, Wonderful Woman of God.*

Trent, John. *Love for All Seasons: Eight Ways to Nurture Intimacy.*

Viscott, David, M.D. *I Love You, Let's Work It Out.*

Wagner, E. Glenn, Ph.D. *Strategies for a Successful Marriage.*

Wheat, Ed, M.D. *How to Save Your Marriage Alone.*

Wheat, Ed, M.D. *Love for Every Married Couple.*

Williamson, Marianne. *A Return to Love.*

Wives of 12 Prominent Christian Leaders. *Promises, Promises.*

Wright, H. Norman. *Quiet Times for Couples: A Daily Devotional.*

Wright, H. Norman. *Always Daddy's Girl.*

Appendix J ~ Tentmakers Missionary Fellowship

419 Mason Street, Suite 215 • Vacaville, CA 95688 • (707) 452-8368

God has a way with people. That's why He's the human resources manager for this organization. In the early days, while the office was a jungle of hanging wires and the furniture was covered with sheetrock dust, He attracted a few people to an idea whose time had come. It was modern tentmaking, a principle of financially supporting the spread of the good news from private means (see Acts 18:2, 3; 20:34; Luke 8:3). Skilled tradespeople and professionals in construction, real estate and ministry began calling or showing up at the office. What they had in common, besides willing hearts, was that they recognized God's scribble on the bottom corner of the blueprint. They knew that the time had come to do the work that God had prepared, and they intuitively knew that somewhere there were others like them.

That's why today, just a few years after its beginning, Tentmakers Missionary Fellowship is partnering with Youth for Christ, Prison Fellowship's Network for Life, many ministries throughout the United States and with local and overseas churches. Wherever the news of this mission spreads, people recognize the signature. God has a creative flourish.

Everyday, Christians are being called by God to join in the work of world evangelization. But some are called specifically, by name, to conduct business "by the Book," wherever they are, so that the name of Jesus receives honor in the workplace. In fact, this model of a holy example is so important that the names of Aquilla and Priscilla, professional tentmakers, were linked to the apostle Paul's ministry in Corinth.

God has already planted in people's hearts (the Aquillas and Priscillas) a readiness to be tentmakers. If you are one of them, you'll recognize the signature.

Please call us, toll free:

1-888-836-8625.

To order additional copies of

Ideas and Suggestions
to Love and Respect
Your Husband

send $ 8.99 plus $ 3.95 for shipping and handling to

Books, Etc.
PO Box 4888
Seattle, WA 98104

or have your credit card ready and call

(800) 917-BOOK

Bulk orders call

Tentmakers Missionary Fellowship

1-888-857-2993
or
1-888-836-8625